The Collected Poems of Katherine Mansfield

Edited by Gerri Kimber and Claire Davison

EDINBURGH
University Press

Edinburgh University Press is one of the leading university presses in the UK.
We publish academic books and journals in our selected subject areas across the
humanities and social sciences, combining cutting-edge scholarship with high editorial
and production values to produce academic works of lasting importance. For more
information visit our website: edinburghuniversitypress.com

Edinburgh University Press Ltd
The Tun - Holyrood Road, 12(2f) Jackson's Entry, Edinburgh EH8 8PJ

Typeset in 10.5/12pt Baskerville MT Pro by
Servis Filmsetting Ltd, Stockport, Cheshire
and printed and bound in Great Britain by
CPI Group (UK) Ltd, Croydon CR0 4YY

A CIP record for this book is available from the British Library

ISBN 978 1 4744 1727 3 (hardback)

Contents

Acknowledgements

We would like to thank the following libraries for permission to use Katherine Mansfield manuscripts held in their possession: the Alexander Turnbull Library, Wellington, New Zealand; the Newberry Library, Chicago, USA; and the Harry Ransom Center, University of Texas at Austin, USA. Special thanks also go to the Society of Authors, which represents the literary estate of Katherine Mansfield, for permission to quote from her work, and in particular, Sarah Burton, for her patience and diligence.

Grateful thanks as always go to our publisher, Jackie Jones, at Edinburgh University Press, whose enthusiasm for our Mansfield projects means so much to us. In addition, we would like to thank the entire team at EUP for their efforts in producing the volume, especially James Dale, Adela Rauchova, Carla Hepburn, Rebecca Mackenzie, and our meticulous copy-editor, Wendy Lee.

We would particularly like to thank Miroslawa Kubasiewicz for helping us to obtain the beautiful cover image by Stanislaw Wyspianski, the talented photographer at Reprezentuj.com, and Father Roman Banasik, the Guardian of St Francis Church, Kraków, Poland, for permission to reproduce it.

Introduction

The big dark house hid secretly
Behind the magnolia and the spreading pear-tree
But there was a sound of music – music rippled and ran
Like a lady laughing behind her fan
Laughing and mocking and running away –
Come into the garden – it's as light as day!

This third stanza from Katherine Mansfield's 1917 poem, 'Night-Scented Stock', is an emblematic example of her poetic voice and style, and thus offers an ideal introduction to our volume – the first stand-alone collected edition of her poetry ever to be published. It brings together all known verse written by Mansfield, from a schoolgirl's first playful experiments in verse in 1903, through to the poignant 'Wounded Bird', written only months before she died from tuberculosis at the age of just thirty-four. Like much of Mansfield's poetry, the above stanza appeals to both the senses – sound, sight and touch – and the sister arts – music, the visual arts and theatre. There is a dignified yet unexplained dramatic setting, with echoes of both mystery and enchantment; worlds intermingle – the secret, dark inner world of a house and the lush, flower-filled natural world outside. A hidden lady's voice resounds enigmatically, inviting someone (the reader perhaps?) to follow, whilst at the same time evading their curiosity, finally departing as abruptly as she appears. The atmosphere conjures up the privileged world of the arts, social glamour and poise, with an added feeling of playfulness, and yet there is a persistent uncomfortable note, suggesting that someone, somewhere, is not quite part of the scene. Linguistically, too, the stanza hovers between two worlds – the heady, exalted idioms of fin-de-siècle decadence and the gentle patter of matter-of-fact colloquialisms. This duality also pervades the poetic idiom – awkward half-rhymes (secretly / pear tree), deadpan monosyllables, lilting yet irregular rhythms, run-on lines and evocative reverberations of words already spoken. Other echoes, too, hover in our minds as we read: the nineteenth-century invitations of Tennyson's 'Come into the garden, Maud'[1], Margaret Richardson's 'The Night Scented Stock', Arthur Symons's 'Stella Maris' or 'White

Heliotrope', but also the gauche self-consciousness of twentieth-century verse such as T. S. Eliot's 'Portrait of a Lady' or 'Conversation Galante'.

However vivid the literary and imaginative resonances may be, the stanza still invites biographical interpretations, as if it were the poetic equivalent of a *roman à clef*. Is the 'spreading pear tree' not an intimate reminder of Mansfield's other memorable pear tree – the one at 5 Acacia Road, St John's Wood, where she had lived just two years before, and which is immortalised at the end of 'Bliss', one of her best-loved short stories? And is this not Garsington, home of the society hostess Ottoline Morrell, where Mansfield had been a guest just at the time the poem was written? Do those shadowy figures not depict the various members of the Bloomsbury set, who all gravitated towards Garsington as a haven for conscientious objectors and pacifists, and a place of rest, employment or feasting in the long war years? This was certainly the impression it made on Morrell herself when, in 1936, she recalled one of her memorable Garsington house-parties, which Mansfield had attended:

> She wrote a little sketch of an evening at Garsington – a hot moon-light night, when we all went into the garden, and some of those who were staying there – amongst them Duncan Grant, David Garnett, Carrington and Gertler – dressed up in fancy clothes, of which I had a store, and danced a lovely wild ballet on the lawn, their white limbs shining in the moonlight against the great elm tree and the dark pond beyond the yew hedges. The music floated out through the windows into the garden. Katherine walked up and down under the house where the night-scented stock had opened its pale flowers, fanning herself with a little black transparent fan and holding it up before her cream face; her eyes, which at times seemed so impenetrable and so opaque that evening, melted and were full of expression.[2]

By the time Morrell was writing, of course, both Mansfield and Garsington were long-lost, fondly cherished recollections of former times. Morrell's imagery suggests she is in part retrieving and rebuilding the past through the language of the poem, as if its evocative scene were shaping and defining memory, rather than the other way round. If real-life settings and biographies are recalled here, they too have been veiled 'behind a fan', and a reader, unfamiliar with the world of artists and intellectuals in 1910s Britain but with a spontaneous, intimate feel for poetry, can be just as moved by the poem's intriguing magic. The rhapsodic excitement woven into the tapestry of talking voices and masked figures leaves a pervading sense that this is a *tableau vivant*, made of dreams, recollections and fantasies, stillness and movement, pose and spontaneity, scraps of conversation, elliptical asides, flashes of description, and heady excitement, but also uneasiness (is this laughing or being laughed at?) and evanescence.

While 'Night-Scented Stock' may reflect the poetic and descriptive poise of a writer who, by 1917, was attaining real maturity, readers of this collection will find the same balancing act, sometimes bold and provocative, sometimes hesitant and whimsical, running throughout the volume. If a division between prose and poetry still makes any sense in the modernist era and after, few writers have made the delicate balance between the two – and between comic patter, pathos, intimacy and parody – such a trademark of their art as Mansfield. Those more familiar with her stories will find the same generic slipperiness and the same disconcerting blend of wonderment, disenchantment, acerbic irony and sharp social commentary running through the poems. Many poems will, in fact, seem to linger on the borders of prose, as if they were short stories in some more condensed form, deliberately constrained in the tighter rhythmic patterns of verse. Others may read like the dénouement of stories – those glimpses of light or obscurity where the narrative breaks off but where some half-hidden truth has been briefly revealed. Readers will find the poems borrowing from various written forms – letters, confessions, prayers, song lines, conversations, dramatic monologues, theatrical scenarios – just as the stories do; likewise, they will find the written voice constantly being shed in favour of a simple spontaneous speaking voice. Indeed, in many cases, Mansfield writes poems for the ear rather than for the eye, taking delight in parodying and pastiching the voices and idioms of an era – expressions characteristic of social, geographic and cultural groupings, or idiosyncratic usage ranging from dialects and solecisms to pretension and ridicule.

Mansfield's readers may also be surprised to see just quite how much verse she wrote in the course of her life. Admittedly, volume 3 of the *Edinburgh Edition of the Collected Works of Katherine Mansfield* brought together all the poems then traced, but the volume also contains all of Mansfield's published non-fiction (book reviews, translations and essays), a godsend for students and scholars, but perhaps less inviting for a reader who wants to settle down in an armchair and enjoy poetry. This is not to mention that more poems came to light even as that volume was being published. Few readers, moreover, are really familiar with any poems beyond the five or six that have been most frequently anthologised in recent years. Very few editions have ever been published; Mansfield's husband, John Middleton Murry, edited a slim volume, *Poems*, in 1923, within a few months of her death, followed by a slightly extended edition in 1930, and Vincent O'Sullivan edited a selection, also titled *Poems*, in 1988. Unsurprisingly, critics and biographers have therefore paid little attention to her poetry, always tending to imply that it was but a minor feature of her art, both in quantity and, more damagingly, in quality. Perhaps one of the most insightful writers on Mansfield to have perceived the intensity and significance of her poetic imagination and composition was her devoted, lifelong friend and companion, Ida Baker. Her intimate recollections of their friendship, *Katherine Mansfield: The Memories of LM* (1971), are peppered with Mansfield's poems, paying proportionally more attention to these than to the stories. It is perhaps one insider's indirect testimony to the importance poetry had in her friend's life and her literary apprenticeship – reminding us of Mansfield's frank admission in her notebook in January 1916: 'I feel always trembling on the brink of poetry.'[3]

Even if Mansfield's poetic output has been traditionally side-lined, many readers of her notebooks, letters and reviews will have noticed that poetry accompanied her throughout her life. A notebook entry from 1915 admits, 'If I lived alone I would be very dependant on poetry.'[4] Increasingly isolated as she spent more and more time abroad, searching for a cure for her tuberculosis, she did indeed come to depend on poetry as a much-valued emotional support. One of her earliest surviving notebooks included a 1903 transcription of a poem by Heine, and, in the same year, on the steamer taking her from New Zealand to Britain for the first time, aged just fifteen, she wrote a verse collection called *Little Fronds*, comprising seventeen poems. Once established at Queen's College, Harley Street, she recorded many of her experiences in poetry and, back in New Zealand three years later, she wrote a book of children's verse, illustrated by a talented young artist called Edith Bendall. The volume was ultimately rejected and the illustrations sadly lost, but the poems survived and are included here, though, unlike *Little Fronds*, no extant manuscript exists and so editorial guesswork has had a hand in the final contents as presented in this volume.

No such problems occur with her poetry cycle, *The Earth Child*, however. The collection was compiled by Mansfield in 1910 and sent to the London publisher, Elkin Mathews, in the second half of that year. It thus represents her second serious attempt at publication of her poetry, this time with far better, more mature verse. No one knew of the manuscript's existence until 1999, when it was bequeathed by the estate of Jane Warner Dick (1906–97) to the Newberry Library in Chicago, where its importance remained unnoticed by scholars until discovered by Gerri Kimber in 2015. Of the thirty-six poems in the collection, only nine had previously been published. The others were completely unknown and yet they represent some of the finest poems Mansfield ever wrote; moreover, they contain information about people, places and events for which almost no other biographical evidence is available. The collection affirms yet again that, although Mansfield was starting to have stories accepted for commercial publication, she was still very much taking herself seriously as a poet.

Moreover, read as a poem-cycle rather than as individual poems, the *Earth Child* sequence acquires a very different literary style and shape. It shows the development of Mansfield's lyrical voice and poetic persona as she moved away from her earlier youthful influences of Oscar Wilde and fin-de-siècle symbolism, towards the more complex neo-Romanticism and early modernism of continental Europe. In addition, it provides a fascinating bridge from those earlier poems, sketches and vignettes through prose-poetry and on to narrative fiction, offering new insights into her evolution and apprenticeship as a writer. As a collection, then, the poems comprise a fascinating record of Mansfield's literary endeavours in 1909–10, as well as offering an incisive illustration of her ability to forge a new literary voice assembled from personal memory, intercultural experimentation and contextual echoes. Had Elkin Mathews published the collection instead of ignoring it, Mansfield might have trod a much more assured – and renowned – poetic literary path.

After the excitement of Mansfield's first real publications of prose-poems and vignettes in Australia and New Zealand in 1907–8, she entered the publishing world in London with verse as well as prose, her poems featuring in a number of key literary and arts reviews, published both in her own name and under pseudonyms such as 'Boris Petrovsky', attesting to the importance she was placing at the time on literature from Central and Eastern Europe. The Slav tone of her pen-name also points to another of Mansfield's major undertakings in the 1910s – her extensive work as a literary reviewer, where we find many examples of her sensitivity as a reader of poetry, and particularly her eloquently expressed belief of how best – and why – poetry should be translated from foreign languages. Nor does she make any bones about disparaging bad poetry or self-indulgent, second-rate versifying. Her review of Kenneth Hare's collection, *Green Fields*, in July 1912 declares:

> The writing of slight verse is the easiest thing in the world – far simpler than the writing of prose – and perhaps it is the most valueless thing in the world. Mr Hare, having nothing to say, says it in rhyme, the which unfortunate state of affairs happens to most young ladies and gentlemen before they have learnt the gentle art of self consciousness.[5]

One of the finest examples of her impatience when faced with weak anthologies occurs in a letter to Murry expressing her irritation with the *Oxford Book of French Verse*: 'But when, in despair I took up the French Book I nearly sautéd from the fenêtre with rage. Its like an endless gallery of French salon furniture sicklied oer with bed canopies, candelabra, and porcelain cupids all bows and bottom.'[6] If such overt criticism also reflects a deep-felt conviction that poetry was a muse to be treated with respect, another fine example of its importance in her eyes can be found in what we might call Mansfield's 'Desert Island Books'. Here was a writer constantly on the move, from one town – indeed, one country – to another, from one form of rented accommodation to another, on and off trains and ships taking her from London to Cornwall, to Paris, to Switzerland, to Germany . . . . The material conditions of travelling, often alone or accompanied only by Ida Baker, would have imposed severe luggage restrictions, yet volumes of poetry are always to be found safely stowed in her bags; judging by her diary entries and lists of belongings to be packed, the *Oxford Book of English Verse* was as faithful a travelling companion as Ida. A volume of Heine, given to her by her childhood sweetheart, Tom (Arnold) Trowell, in 1903, also crops up regularly in her lists of her recorded reading.

Reading notes which list the poetry she was reading also remind readers how very well read Mansfield was, and offer a first indication of the lasting influence of poetic styles and idioms, echoes of which can then be traced back through her own work. Rarely are these explicit references; they are resonances and half-allusions pointing to the literary recollections buzzing round her mind, which then resurface and enrich the intertextual tapestry of her own textual production. As the various notes here will indicate to those readers wanting to look further into the poetic sources that linger on from her mind to her verse, there are striking echoes of Hardy, Blake, Symons, Whitman, Wordsworth, Coleridge, Tennyson and Dowson, to name a few of the English-language influences; the European voices include Goethe, Heine, Wyspianski, Mallarmé, Baudelaire and Carco. Nor are these fleeting allusions restricted to the canonical or 'serious' poets. Mansfield's sense of poetic pastiche can recall Lear and Belloc; she can interweave uplifting snatches from popular hymns and *The Book of Common Prayer*, and set these alongside traditional nursery rhymes and sing-song ballads, before shifting just as suddenly, to tones reminiscent of some of the contemporary poets of her era – John Davidson and 'the Rhymers', Walter de la Mare and T. S. Eliot.

Here is perhaps one of the greatest challenges of reading Mansfield's verse: the beguiling simplicity that contains so much. Much of her poetry is, of course, autobiographical and personal, but, as another diary entry from 1921 reveals, it can also serve as an escape from the immediacies of life and personality: 'Oh God! I am divided still. I am bad. I fail in my personal life. I lapse into impatience, temper, vanity & so I fail as thy priest. Perhaps poetry will help.'[7] Her own verse is richly evocative of the poetic works she absorbs, with lingering memories of cherished lines, images and styles, but also it is always, unmistakably, her voice that we are hearing.

Thus this volume deserves to be read as a superb testimony to Mansfield's own development as a writer. Often her poetry can mark some sort of alchemy, as sights, sounds and memories are transmuted into literature; similarly, many of her stories can be seen to start life as intensely poetic moments that gradually expand just enough to push poetry beyond its own constraints of rhyme and rhythm into prose. The hallmarks of her very best fiction are all to be found in condensed form in verse – her focus on the telling detail that captures some essential flavour or feel of a scene, the swift, sure strokes of a description that capture beauty or idiosyncratic quirks. In many poems, just as in the stories, diction and form are often simple and traditional: floating trochees, sing-song iambics, a certain sentimental sweetness that might just appear too cloying. But even the naïve effects can prove sophisticated, reflecting a denser poetic fabric beneath the apparent simplicity: strong, regular metres suddenly slipping into free-running lines, crisp social niceties that change tune midway, predictable patterns that are suddenly transformed by casually thrown in hiatuses and subdued climaxes, flat-footed commonplaces and playful nonsense rhymes that abruptly acquire sinister overtones, and lyricism or fey innocence that carefully hides an underside that is *faux-naïf* or positively wicked.

And these connections matter – Mansfield's poetic art may lie in briefly surveyed scenes, passing voices and imagist-type glimpses, but they constantly connect to the wider socio-political realities around her. Hers is a poetic voice that requires us to rethink the lyric, and recall that, across the centuries, lyric poetry has never been synonymous with simply 'being lyrical'. Even when Mansfield's immediate subject matter may be mere snippets of everyday life, and even when the poetic voice appears to be laughing, her 'cry against corruption'[8] is still clamouring to be heard: war, the condition of women and other socially marginalised groups, poverty, class consciousness, sickness, bereavement – these themes too can provide the stuff her poetry is made on. Such poems share resonances with poets like Arthur Symons, but also with her own unmistakable prose and its clear preoccupation with underworlds – the marginal lives on the streets of London, the likely plight of lone women, the economic vulnerability of musicians and traders, the thrill and the solitude of constantly changing places.

Every reader will find their own entry into this volume. Some might start from the beginning and work methodically through to the end; others might start with their own particular favourites and work out from there; others still may just dip in as the fancy takes them and see what they find. All such approaches are to be defended and will yield surprising, yet very different impressions. However, a word or two may be useful to indicate how we have arranged the volume. The poems have been organised chronologically as far as possible. We have drawn on archive sources, letters and notebook dating, and have paid close attention to references within the texts that can help date poems when no other indications were available. Vigilant as we have been, this chronology cannot be taken as absolute. As is well known, Mansfield never started her notebooks at the beginning to end at the end. Her constant travels meant she would have several notebooks half-filled at hand, and drafts clearly begin when and wherever she finds a convenient space – which can include turning an exercise book upside down to work in the other direction, or returning years later to an old book to note down a series of lines or rhymes on an available blank page. Beyond the eventual misdating of poems that such haphazard usage may lead to, there are other factors that have sometimes meant the overall chronological order has been broken. The key example here is that of the three poetry collections that Mansfield assembled for publication together, when, in each case, we chose to keep the collection intact (with the caveat as noted above concerning the child-verse collection), thereby giving readers an indication of the projected volume's internal chronology. The three collections are *Little Fronds* (1903), a children's book of verse (1907) and the recently rediscovered poetry cycle, *The Earth Child* (1910); it is the latter collection, in particular, which reveals just how essential internal cohesion would prove to be for Mansfield, as explained above.

Another factor which influenced the layout of this volume is that of annotations. We believe our notes are an essential reader's tool, pointing to cultural details, source references, likely allusions and useful reverberations with other works by Mansfield. As we discovered time and again, Mansfield was a prodigiously well-read writer, and her poetry bears the stamp of a subtle intellectual mind as much as it reflects her poignantly short but eventful life. The notes therefore attempt to draw attention to as many of the intertextual resonances as possible, in the hope that these leads can inspire future generations of readers, students and scholars who might, in turn, follow up and explore the allusions in greater depth. However, notes can sometimes impede reading more than they enhance it. Poetry, after all, is more about loving words and revelling in their sounds and shapes than providing a dense crossword puzzle to be deciphered. For this reason, the notes have been kept at the back of the volume, so that readers who would much rather let their imagination and their senses hold sway as they read, can do just that.

Notes

For a full list of abbreviations used here, readers should refer to the main 'Notes' section at the end of the volume, on page 142.

1. As this line emphasises, there are resonances throughout the poem, and particularly in this verse, to Alfred Tennyson's famous song, 'Come into the garden, Maud' from his extended poem-cycle, 'Maud' (1855).
2. Helen Shaw, ed., *Dear Lady Ginger: An Exchange of Letters Between Lady Ottoline Morrell and D'Arcy Cresswell* (Oxford: Oxford University Press, 1983), p. 124.
3. CW4, p. 192.
4. CW4, p. 148.
5. CW3, p. 431.
6. L1, p. 205, to JMM (9 December 1915).
7. CW4, p. 208.
8. L2, p. 54, to JMM (3 February 1918).

1903

Collection: *Little Fronds*

Evening

Evening is come
The glory of the sunset
Floods the sky
The little birds lift up their evening hymns
To God on High.

But one by one
The colours now have faded
The sky grows gray
No star is seen in all the heavens to guide us
If we should stray.

At last, one wee star peeps from out its covert
Of the now darkened sky
To cheer the rough and stony way before us
For you and I.

It is a narrow path that lies before us
And difficult and winding is the way,
Almighty Guide, watch over us and shield us
Lest we should stray.

The Sea

O the beauty, O the grandeur of the sea
What stories does its changeful visage tell
To you and me.

When fiercely rage the tempests o'er the deep
And all the slumb'ring world is waked from sleep

When the sea sobs, as if in sad distress
And none are there to cheer my loneliness
I feel for thee O Sea.

In calm and tempest and in storm and strife
In all the bitter changeful scenes of life
In death's dark hour before Eternity
I feel for thee, O Sea.

The Three Monarchs

Day took off her azure mantle
She laid down her golden crown
And she sank to her rest on the cloudlets
On pillows of rosy down.

Twilight, clad in a sombre mantle
Ascended the vacant throne
His face was haggard and weary
And his courtiers left him alone.

When the reign of Twilight was over
Night, clad in a robe of black
Saw the far away form of the monarch
And beckoned to him to come back.

But twilight, his course pursuing
Ne'er turned, ne'er lifted his head
And the face of Night grew despairing
In low hollow tones he said

Alas! Alas! where are my brethren?
Am I left here alone to die?
Does no one care for my welfare
When I on my deathbed lie?

And he wrapt his robe around him
And down in the darkness he lay
The reign of the night was over
And back to her throne came Day.

Music

The world began with music,
Wist ye not the 'Music of the Spheres'

And the angels will be playing harps of gold
When Judgement Day appears.

When Christ our Heavenly Lord came down to earth
And solemn stillness reignèd all around
A burst of angels song proclaimed his birth
That made the whole world tremble at the sound – – –

We pray that when our Lord may come again
And when we hear that angels music ring
That we may shout with one accord 'Amen'
And with the angels joyfully may sing.

All the world is music
Wist ye not the music of the sea
The music of the birds, the winds, the flowers
'Tis all in all to me.

A Fragment

What thing, more beautiful, more fair
To eyes of God and man is
Than a garden.

It is the spot where
Man first prayed to God
Craving his pardon.

Love's Entreaty

Lovest thou me, or lovest me not
Whisper and do not fear
Let me not wait thine answer, love
The time to part draws near.

Why standest thou, so proud, so cold
Would I thy heart might see
The moon shall wane, and the stars grow old
Ere I lose my love for thee.

If thou wouldst take my heart, my life
If I thy slave might be
I'd reck not for the world's hard strife
O my love, I would live for thee.

Night

When the shadows of evening are falling
And the world is preparing for sleep
When the birds to their wee ones are calling
And the stars are beginning to peep

A peace steals into my heart
Which no one and nothing can break
And I from my old sorrows part
Till the morrow begins to awake.

O night, how I love and adore thee
Why dost thou so short a time stay
My sorrows come crowding back o'er me
When the shades of the night pass away.

I hope I may die in the darkness
When the world is so quiet and so still
And my soul pass away with the shadows
Ere the sun rises over the hill.

To M

For me, O love, thine eyes like stars are shining
For me, thy voice is all the sound I need
O love, dear love, dost know how I am pining
My heart to plead.

The world goes on, with tears and with laughter
I care not for the world, I care for thee
I care not for this life and what comes after
'Tis nought to me.

O love, dear love, thou art my soul, thy presence
Is aught that e'er can soothe my aching heart
Wilt thou not give me but one word of comfort
Before we part.

Thou'rt going, and the light from out my life is dying
It flickers and ere long it shall be dead
And I shall try to follow, blind with crying
Where thou hast led.

Battle Hymn

Fight on, weary pilgrims, fight
Soon or late there shall be light
Struggle then, with main and might
Till the glass grows clear.

Be not weary, seek not rest
For to fight is to be blest
And your victories He shall test
When the glass grows clear.

Like your leader strive to be
Perfect, without fault is He
And his greatness we shall see
When the glass grows clear.

The Chief's Bombay Tiger

Since leaving New Zealand
I grieve to say
A great Bombay tiger
Has come to stay.

He is kept by the chief
In the No. 2 hold
And is famous for doing
Whatever he's told.

And at night when the ladies
Have gone to bed
This great Bombay tiger
Prowls round overhead.

At six and seven, he's heard to roar
At the ladies' porthole or cabin door
But the lady passengers venture to say
They never feel safe till that tiger's away.

Now your pardon I beg, dear chief, to intrude
And if you don't think me most horribly rude
Just keep your dear tiger in No. 2 hold
And your pardon I beg for being so rude.

To Ping Pong by J. E. C.

Ping Pong, thy charms have captured ladies fair
Thou'rt spoken of by all the statesmen rare
Cupid and bow and arrows, these are thine
Ping Pong hast captured e'en this heart of mine.

I care not for the charms of playing whist
A game of billiards I can't well resist
But if I see a ping pong ball and bat
Why man, I cry, the game's not worth your hat.

Give me a table and a green baize net
A ball, a racquet, and a girl I met
I am content to play all day and night
Until I've lost my breath and lost my sight.

To a Little Child

Sleep on, little one
All is well.
Better to die thus
Than go to Hell.

Life is but cold and hard
Death is sweet
Many the traps are set
For wandering feet.

Would I could die as thou
Hast done this day
In childish faith and love
Be ta'en away.

Rest, my little one
Flowers on your breast
Safe in the cold earth's arms
Ever at rest.

In the Darkness

I am sitting in the darkness
And the whole house is still
But I feel I need your presence
Since I've been ill.

It was different in the Springtime
Different then, when all was right
But when all the world is darkness
When all the world is night

O my darling then I want you
For I know you understand
And I yearn to feel your presence
And to feel you clasp my hand.

When I first was told my sorrow
Told that I could never more
See the gay world and the sunshine
As I always had before

O, I thought I could not bear it
Bear to live and to be blind
But the thought of your great absence
Drove all else from out my mind.

And I thought and thought about you
Would you sorrow? Would you care?
When you heard that I was blinded
And was left to linger here?

I am lonely in the darkness
All the world seems dull and still
And my friends have all forgot me
Since I've been ill.

The Springtime

O, a Queen came to visit our country
She was young, and was loved by us all
How we hailed the glad signs of her coming
When we first heard the merry thrush call.

And the flowers sprang up to peep at her
And the trees shook their young leaves with joy
And the daisies came out for her carpet
And she came to us, smiling and coy.

E'en the sun stayed to watch her and court her
How we wished she would stay here for aye
But, alas, she grew tired of our revels
And Queen Springtime soon vanished away.

To Grace

When shall I tell you it
Shall it be at night
When the soft wind kisses you
And the stars are bright

Or tell it in the twilight
When the shadows fall
And I still can see your face
Your face, loved best of all.

What matter when I tell you it
Though the fact is shocking
I'll tell you ere my courage fails
'There's a big hole in your stocking.'

Hope

Life is hard
But let us hope
And to live will bring less pain
Let us not in darkness grope
Hope again.

We are tired
But let us hope
And our rest will be more calm
Let us cling fast to life's rope
Safe from harm.

Farewell

Dear little book, farewell
I have loved thee long
Bright may your future be
Like a spring song.

Oft thou hast cheerèd me
When I was sad
When I was all alone
Thou made me glad.

Dear little book, farewell
I have loved thee long

With thee, my childish thoughts
Are ever gone.

Collection Ends

An Escapade Undertaken by A Green Raspberry, & A Kidney Bean

The shades of night had fallen fast
When from Miss Wood's two spirits passed
Two girls, who bore a worried look
And muttered as their way they took
Miss Harper

Their brows were sad their eyes were bright
As stars upon a summer night
But as they clambered down the stairs
They both repeated unawares
Miss Harper

Beware pneumonia's dreadful pain
Beware the drafts that kill your frame
This was their guardian's last goodnight
Their voices rang out clear and bright
Miss Harper.

O stay, the girls said, do not go
Pray stay awhile and let us sew
They turned away with maddened looks
And sang out as they took their books
Miss Harper

At break of day did Alfred leap
To light the fires and dust and sweep
He whistled loud he whistled clear
Voices rose from the thick atmosphere
Miss Harper

Two girls asleep in the office chair
waked by Miss Harper who found them there
Look up at her with sleepy eyes
And mutter – with a vague surprise
Miss Harper

Twilight

Twilight is gathering round us, dearest,
It is the end of this short day

And our lives have come to the twilight, dearest,
You and I have not long to stay.

Come, stand by me at the window, dearest
Look out at the calm, quiet sky.

The Old Inkstand

O, the old inkstand on the table stays
It is too shabby to sell
In truth it has seen much better days
It has many a story to tell.

There was a time when its drawers were full
Of red wax and old quill pens

Friendship

He sat by his attic window
The moonlight was streaming
Over his furrowed face
He had sat thus for hours with his head bent
Never moving his place.

He thought of the long past sweetness
When life had started
Like a blossoming rose
Of how soon it had spent all its beauty and fragrance
And gone – no man knows

He thought of his future before him
The figure of poverty
Looked in his eyes
He saw his old friends watch him begging and praying
With silent surprise.

Friendship (2)

He sat at his attic window
The night was bitter cold
But he did not seem to feel it
He was so old – so old –

The moonlight silvered his grey hair
And caressed his furrowed face
The clock at the old church tower struck twelve
But he did not change his place.

He thought of his happy boyhood
How life had seemed to him
Like an ever dancing river
And his eyes grew misty and dim

Then he thought of his dismal Future
Alone, and loved by none
Dark clouds lay in every direction
And hid the glorious sun.

He moaned as he sat at the window
And moved as though in pain
'O dream of my happy boyhood
Come back to me again.' – – –

Suddenly all his attic
Was lit with wondrous light
And there stood up before him
Figures from out the night.

Lo, they were five young maidens
And they stood before him all
As though 'twere the richest castle
And his room a banqueting hall

And he said in low strained accents
'What would ye have with me
For I am poor and aged
And have not heard of thee'.

And the maidens sang together
'Hear us you poor old man
We have come to blight your troubles
And help you if we can.

Know then our names are beauty,
Youth, friendship, riches and peace

And we would make you happy
And cause your pain to cease.

Choose one of us, choose wisely
That whom thou lovest best
She will remain with you always
Until your eternal rest.'

Then the maidens stopped their singing
'If my sorrow would find release
I must choose that which is most perfect
And her beautiful name is *Peace*'.

Then before his weary vision
The spirits faded fast
But Peace stayed still beside him
And held him to her, fast.

They found him the next morning
Quite dead upon the floor
The old man had ah, truly
Found Peace for evermore.

The Song of my Lady

My lady sits and sings
The sunlight flings
Its beams, and brings
Ripe gold into her hair –
O my lady, knowing nothing
Fearing nothing, she sits there.

My lady sits and sighs
The autumn wind
Not overkind
Tries to unbind
Her golden hair –
O my lady, knowing all things
Fearing many, has learnt Care.

My lady sits and sews
The broidery grows
Like a summer rose
She little knows
She's aught to fear –
O my lady, be more watchful
Do not sit so blindly there!

The Old Year and the New Year

Tonight we passed a Milestone on the road
One nearer to the great one and the last
Slowly we tread, for heavier grows our load
And veils of mist are creeping o'er the Past.

One Milestone nearer! do we understand
We pass so many; sometimes we forget,
We have crept closer to the dear Lord's hand
Are we quite ready to receive it yet?

The night is dark; our way is hard to find
We stumble and alas! we often fall
But we have God to pity and to bind
Our wounds, if only we but faintly call.

O God, our Father, be with us tonight
And listen while to thee we feebly pray
Let there be all around us a great Light
Turning our darkness into brightest day.

1904

'This is my world, this room of mine'

This is my world, this room of mine
Here I am living – – – and here I shall die
All my interests are here, in fine
– – – The hours slip quickly by.

Look on these shelves – just books, you would say
Friends I can tell you, one and all
Most of them sorrowful – some of them gay – –
And my pictures that line the wall.

Yes, that is a Doré, from where I sit
At night with my books or my work, I see
The light that falls and glorifies it – – –
And I gaze and it strengthens me.

Ah! in this cupboard, my miser's store
Of music finger it sheaf on sheaf
Elixir of life – – it is something more
It is Heaven to me, in brief.

And that is my 'cello, my all in all
Ah, my beloved, quiet you stand
– – – If I let the bow ever so softly fall,
– – – The magic lies under my hand.

And on winter nights when the fire is low
We comfort each other, till it would seem
That the night outside, all cold and snow
Is the ghost of a long past dream.

This is my world, this room of mine
Here I am living – – – here I shall die
All my interests are here in fine
– The hours slip quickly by.

22

'Dear friend'

Dear friend, when back to Canada you go
And leave old England far away behind
When in the dark storms, in the bitter snow
You hug your fire, with a quiet mind

Think of the bathroom, warm and filled with light
With strains of 'Orchid' and sweet music rare
And Norway singing songs with all her might
– Then wish that you could be transported there.

Dear friend, when back to Canada you go
And taste once more the sweet delights of home
Do not forget us who have loved you so
And think of us, wherever you may roam.

1906

'What, think you, causes me truest Joy'

What, think you, causes me truest joy
Down by the sea – the wild mad storm of waves
the fierce rushing swirl of waters together
The cruel salt spray that blows, that beats upon my face.
Wet grey sand, straight paths of it, leading far and away
And showing never a sign of where man's foot has trod
Till only the sky overhead peers at itself in the mirror
The flying clouds, silently screaming, shudder and gaze at themselves
– – –

The song of the wind as I stretch out my arms and embrace it
This indeed gives me joy.

The Students' Room

In the students' room the plain and simple beds
The pictures that line the walls, of various excellence thrown together
And the students with heads bent low, silent over their books.

'To those who can understand her'

To those who can understand her
London means everything.
Black buds in the Times [?] Square garden
Can herald a glorious Spring.
Oh the park! in the early morning.
You can hear the robin sing.

A Common Ballad

Outside is the roar of London town
But we have pulled the sun blinds down
And are as snug as snug can be
Chaddie and me.

She lying on the empty bed
Her book half covering up her head
And *very* much 'en déshabille'
Chaddie – *not* me.

I – sitting here to write to you
And looking like a stocking blue
We both are longing for our tea
Chaddie and me.

But we're not really learned tho'
This poem sounds as if we're so
And with our grammar we're most free
Chaddie and me.

Our sister – with her face all red
Has gone to see her Ma instead
Well – she is she, and we are we
Chaddie and me.

Far better here to quietly stay
And eat and yawn away the day
We'll end by going to the d – – –
Chaddie and me.

She now is very fast asleep
God grant her hair in waves will keep
But no one is so sweet as we
Chaddie and me.

'I constantly am hearing'

I constantly am hearing
A cry, a muffled groan
A voice deep and despairing
Is Ethel all alone –

All alone Ethel
It sounds quite like a song

You will be hearing Melisand
Before so very long

But is the heart of every man
Become so like a stone
That he [. . .]
While Ethel's all alone?
I constantly am hearing.

Oft in the stilly Night
Ere slumbers chains have bound me
My sleep is put to flight
By all the noise around me.

Along the corridor
Strange gurgles, many a sound.

Shadows

Shadows of days long past,
Your voices are clear!
And soft as the wind through the new leafed tree.
And the sound of your singing comes to me
Through the long sweet grass O I can faintly hear
Shadows of days long past . . .

Shadows of days long past,
Come back again!
Never again – ah me! – the leaves may fall
Soft o'er the grass, and the Winter Pall
Darken the world – I shall call you in vain –
Shadows of days long past!

Ah! the Dream days of my Youth –
Gone from my ken.
Yet some day I hope when the Night draws down
I may meet you again in Shadow Town
Forgetting this world of women and men
Shadows of days long past . . .

The [. . .] Child of the Sea

Here in the sunlight wild I lie
Wrapt up warm with my pillow and coat
Sometimes I look at the big blue sky

The wide grey sky, the wide grey sky
And ever the clouds move slowly by
The fierce shrill note of the sea-birds' cry
Here in my strange bed.

The endless sea, the endless sea
And the song that is sung repeatedly
In every rhythm and time and theme
Till I shriek aloud . . . but it deafens me.

The changing light, the changing light
Purple and gold change to the night
A wide strong blue when the sun is bright
A riot of colour – a wonder sight.

Valley and hill, valley and hill
I am swept along – I never am still
I have cried, I have cursed, I have prayed my fill.

It carries me near the loved one.

Here we
And the shivering song of the poplars
And away in the distance the sea.

1907

Collection: Children's Book of Verse

Verses of Little Q

If you have never been a girl
You cannot know the sin
To wear just 'dress material'
To keep your 'bodies' in.

An' I shall never quite forget
The feeling that I felt
When Mother went and bought for me
A Ladies' Leather Belt.

One Day

One dreadful day, you hurried in,
And 'Half-past-five', you said,
'The Smiths is runnin after me
And says my hair is *red*!'

The Smiths *had* been great friends of mine
That feeling all was gone –
'It's just a halo, dear,' I cried
'God *always* has one on!'

'The little boy'

The little boy went to sleep in the car
The journey had been too long.
He hadn't a notion that home was so far
The little boy went to sleep in the car.

'The sunlight shone in golden beams'

The sunlight shone in golden beams
Across my lonely way
But I was wrapped in youthful dreams
And did not say them nay.

If Mother and Father were left to themselves
And hadn't a baby to play with
Suppose now we left you alone on the street
For someone to just run away with.

I really can't think what we both would be at
Two grumbly old nasty old cronies
And never the sound of a young lady's feet
To make us not feel by our lonies

I think that we'd have to buy something instead
A nice little dog or a kitten
A nice little persian haired round little puss
Not the family who would lose their mitten.

But really we'd both of us feel very sad
And quite wash our eyes out with water
And sit very close and exclaim all the time
If we only had that little daughter.

A Young Ladies Version of The Cards

Diamonds are for grown up ladies
Clubs for Giants fierce and tall
Spades for digging the garden
But Hearts are meant for all –
O but Hearts are meant for all.

The Bath Baby

Fair Water Nymph, I pray of you
Don't splash the water so
Although I'm sure it's lovely to
Make big waves with your toe.

Six o'clock is bathing time,
Bring the tub and bring the water

Spread the big mat on the floor
Run and fetch the little daughter.

When you've got on your party frock,
We really think you sweet
And even in a pinafore
You're very clean and neat.

But O the time we love you best
Is – by the Nursery hearth
With just your little nakeds on
And splashing in the bath.

It's quite the most important thing
That happens in the day
When you have sat on Daddy's knee
And quite forgot to play

And feel your head go noddy nod
And almost 'clined to cry
Then Mummy says – come precious one
It's time for bedy bye.

She takes you from your comfy place
Your warm and cosy nest
And pops off all your clothes until
You've only just a vest.

So back you creep to Daddykin
He gives your toes a rub
While Mummy puts the bath mat down
And fetches in the tub.

And sponge and soap and powder box
(The dear soft fluffy puffs)
And Mummy ties her apron on
And pushes up her cuffs.

The towels are spread before the fire
And Mummy pins your hair
And then she does your hair on top
In one big wobbly curl
And says now run along jump in
O *what* a lucky girl.

To get in right all by yourself's
The hardest thing of all.
The water looks so big and hot
And O – you feel so small.

But when you're soaped from top to toe
All lovely frothy white
You feel you never can get out
But just stay there all night

And [she] puts the sponge right in your mouth
And makes the waves go by
[. . .] takes you, rolls you up
You haven't time to cry.

It seems to you she rubs too hard
You cry O that's enough.
And then the cloud of powder comes
You love the powder puff.

And while she pops your Nighty on
And puts away your clothes
You pull your Daddy down quite close
And powder all *his* nose.

'This is just a little song'

This is just a little song
That a child once sang to me.
(O the bitter years and long
Since she sat upon my knee.)
Mother when we take a walk, you and I along the
Shore I can scarcely ever talk.
                              *

O Mother Mine, O mother mine
Snuggle me close and hold me fast
When will the weather again be fine
Shall I really get well at last?

'I have a little garden plot'

I have a little garden plot
That Daddy gave to me
And there I grow forgetmenot
And radishes for tea.

And pansies for my Mother dear

Grace before meat.

A Fine Day

After all the rain, the sun
Shines on hill and grassy mead
Fly into the garden, child,
You are very glad indeed.

For the days have been so dull,
Oh, so special dark and drear,
What you told me, 'Mr. Sun
Has forgotten we live here.'

Dew upon the lily lawn
Dew upon the garden beds
Daintily from all the leaves
Pop the little primrose heads.

And the violets in the copse
With their parasols of green
Take a little 'peek' at you
They're the bluest you have seen.

On the lilac tree a bird
Singing first a little note
Then a burst of happy song
Bubbles in his lifted throat.

O, the Sun, the comfy Sun!
This the song that you must sing,
'Thank you for the birds, the flowers,
Thank you, Sun, for everything.'

A New Hymn

Sing a song of men's pyjamas,
Half-past-six has got a pair,
And he's wearing them this evening,
And he's looking *such* a dear.

Sing a song of frocks with pockets
I have got one, it is so's
I can use my 'nitial hankies
Every time I blow my nose.

The Black Monkey

My Babbles has a nasty knack
Of keeping monkeys on her back.
A great big black one comes and swings
Right on her sash or pinny strings.
It is a horrid thing and wild
And makes her such a naughty child.

She comes and stands beside my chair
With almost an offended air
And says: – 'Oh, Father, why can't I?'
And stamps her foot and starts to cry –
I look at Mother in dismay . . .
What little girl is this, to-day?

She throws about her nicest toys
And makes a truly dreadful noise
Till Mother rises from her place
With quite a Sunday churchy face
And Babbles silently is led
Into the dark and her own bed.

Never a kiss or one Goodnight,
Never a glimpse of candle light.
Oh, how the monkey simply flies!
Oh, how poor Babbles calls and cries,
Runs from the room with might and main
'Father dear, I am good again.'

When she is sitting on my knee
Snuggled quite close and kissing me,
Babbles and I, we think the same –
Why, that the monkey *never* came
Only a terrible dream maybe . . .
What did she have for evening tea?

The Family

Hinemoa, Tui, Maina,
All of them were born together
They are quite an extra special
Set of babies – wax and leather.

Every day they took an airing
Mummy made them each a bonnet

Two were cherry, one was yellow
With a bow of ribbon on it.

Really, sometimes we would slap them
For if ever we were talking
They would giggle and be silly,
Saying, 'Mamma, take us walking.'

But we never really loved them
Till one day we left them lying
In the garden – through a hail-storm
And we heard the poor dears crying.

Half-past-six said – 'You're a mother
What if Mummy did forget *you*?'
So I said, 'Well, you're their Father
Get them' but I wouldn't let you.

'When I was little'

When I was quite a little child
Just three o'clock or even less –
I always fell and hurt my knees,
And *once* I tore my party dress.

It's such an awful thing to do
Because folks say: – '*What not again!*'
I wish they'd do it by themselves
And feel perhaps, the awful pain.

I used to creep away and think –
'I'll die today, to make them sad'
The tears came always rushing down,
Because I felt so very bad.

But when my daddy found me there
And kissed me – heaps of times – you know
I used to say – 'Perhaps then, dads –
I'll live another day or so.'

The Clock

The clock is always going round,
It never stops, it always goes –

And makes a funny little sound
What does it say – do you suppose?

I stand upon my 'special' chair
When Nurse has cleared away the tea
And see its big white face quite near –
With little marks like 'A.B.C.'

You're half-past-six – I'm half-past-five,
O dear, how very old we are
I wonder if we'll stay alive
Like Santa Claus and Grandmamma?

Before I go to bed at night
Or say my 'Lead me into Heaven'
I kiss the clock with all my might
And whisper – 'Make us eight and seven'.

The Letter

Dear Half-past-six you know
I can't get out of bed
I sat in wet feet – so
A cold is in my head.

I've got three blankets on
As hot as hot can be
The doctor has just gone
I'm ninety-nine, point three.

He told my Mummy it
I heard him – by the door
But it's not true, a bit,
I'm half-past five, no more.

What *would* he say you were
Could you be more than me?
A *billion* p'raps – now dear
Goodbye, here comes my tea.

The Birthday Present

Granny taught us how to make them
'Knit two plain and then two pearl'

It is not so very easy
Even if you are a girl.

But I think cuffs are so useful
They are not so very big,
Cook told me they looked like waist bands
But we *said* she was a pig.

They are grey – the colour's pretty
Don't go thinking they were white
I told daddy he was foolish
He said, 'Half-past-five, you're right.'

If they won't keep on you now please
Save them till we're married – for
You can't then be buying new things
And your hands will grow much more.

The Pillar Box

The pillar box is fat and red,
The pillar box is high;
It has the flattest sort of head
And not a nose or eye,
But just one open nigger mouth
That grins when I go by.

The pillar box is very round
But hungry all the day;
Although it doesn't make a sound,
Folks know it wants to say,
'Give me some letter sandwiches
To pass the time away.'

'A postage stamp I like to eat
Or gummy letterette.'
I see the people on the street,
If it is fine or wet,
Give something to the greedy thing;
They never quite forget.

The pillar box is quite a friend
When Father goes away,
My Mother has such lots to send,
Fat letters every day,
And so I drop them in its mouth
When I go out to play.

Song by the Window Before Bed

Little star, little star
Come down. Quick.
The Moon is a Bogey-man
He'll catch you certain if he can.
Little star, little star
Come down quick.

Little star, little star
Whisper 'Yes.'
The trees are just niggers all
They look so black, they are so tall.
Little star, little star
Whisper 'Yes.'

Little star, little star,
Gone – all gone –
The Bogey-man swallowed you
The nigger trees are laughing, too
Little star, little star
Gone – all gone.

The Funeral

It was Mr Lun's 'At Home' day
So of course he never came
But it didn't make much difference
We *was* happy all the same.

And just sittin' by the window
With what Mummy calls 'the blue'
When we saw a lovely funeral
Comin' up our own street, too.

All the horses wore a bonnet
With a wobbly curly feather

A Little Boy's Dream

To and fro, to and fro
In my little boat I go
Sailing far across the sea
All alone – just little me

And the sea is big and strong
And the journey very long
To and fro, to and fro
In my little boat I go.

Sea and sky, sea and sky.
Quietly on the deck I lie
Having just a little rest.
I have really done my best
In an awful Pirate Fight,
But we captured them all right.
Sea and sky, sea and sky
Quietly on the deck I lie.

Far away, far away
From my home and from my play
On a journey without end
Only with the sea for friend
And the fishes in the sea
But they swim away from me
Far away, far away
From my home and from my play.

Then he cried 'O *Mother* dear'
And he woke and sat upright.
They were in the rocking chair,
Mother's arms around him – tight.

Winter Song

Rain and wind, and wind and rain
Will the Summer come again?
Rain on houses, on the street
Wetting all the people's feet
Though they run with might and main
Rain and wind and wind and rain.

Snow and sleet and sleet and snow.
Will the Winter never go?
What do beggar children do
With no fire to cuddle to
P'raps with nowhere warm to go?
Snow and sleet and sleet and snow.

Hail and ice, and ice and hail,
Water frozen in the pail

See the robins brown and red
They are waiting to be fed
Poor dears! battling in the gale
Hail and ice and ice and hail.

On a Young Lady's Sixth Anniversary

Baby Babbles – only *one* –
Now to sit up has begun.

Little Babbles quite turned *two*
Walks as well as I and you.

And Miss Babbles *one two three*
Has a teaspoon at her tea.

But her Highness at *four*
Learns to open the front door.

And her Majesty – now *six*
Can her shoestrings neatly fix.

Babbles, Babbles – have a care
You will soon *put up your hair*!

Song of the Little White Girl

Cabbage Tree, Cabbage Tree – what is the matter –
Why are you shaking so, why do you chatter?
'Cause it is just a white baby you see –
And it's the black ones you like – Cabbage Tree?
Cabbage Tree, Cabbage Tree – you're a strange fellow
With your green hair and your legs browny-yellow
Wouldn't you like to have curls, dear, like me?
What! no-one to make them – O *poor* Cabbage Tree!
Never mind, Cabbage Tree – when I am taller
And if you grow – please – a little bit smaller
I shall be able by that time – may be –
To make you the loveliest curls, Cabbage Tree.

A Few Rules for Beginners

Babies must not eat the coal
And they must not make grimaces

Nor in party dresses roll
And must never black their faces.

They must learn that 'pointing's' rude
They must sit quite still at table
And must always eat the food
Put before them – if they're able.

If they fall, they must not cry
Though it's known how painful this is
Lo – there's always Mother by
Who will comfort them with kisses.

A Day in Bed

I wish I had not got a cold;
    The wind is big and wild;
I wish that I was very old,
    Not just a little child.

Somehow the day is very long,
    Just keeping here alone.
I do not like the big wind's song,
    He's growling for a bone.

He's like an awful dog we had
    Who used to creep around
And snatch at things – he was so bad –
    With just that horrid sound.

I'm sitting up and Nurse has made
    Me wear a woolly shawl -
I wish I was not so afraid:
    It's horrid to be small.

It really feels quite like a day
    Since I have had my tea;
P'raps everybody's gone away,
And just forgotten me.

And, oh, I cannot go to sleep,
    Although I am in bed;
The wind keeps going 'creepy-creep'
    And waiting to be fed.

Opposites

The Half-Soled-Boots-With-Toecaps-Child,
Walked out into the street,
And splashed in all the puddles till
She had such shocking feet.

The Patent-Leather-Slipper-Child
Stayed quietly in the house
And sat upon the fender stool
As still as any mouse.

The Half-Soled-Boots-With-Toecaps-Child
Her hands were black as ink
She would come rushing through the house
And begging for a drink.

The Patent-Leather-Slipper-Child,
Her hands were white as snow,
She did not like to play around
She only liked to sew.

The Half-Soled-Boots-With-Toecaps-Child,
Lost hair ribbons galore,
She dropped them on the garden walks,
She dropped them on the floor.

The Patent-Leather-Slipper-Child,
O, thoughtful little girl,
She liked to walk quite soberly,
It kept her hair in curl.

The Half-Soled-Boots-With-Toecaps-Child
When she was glad or proud
Just flung her arms round Mother's neck
And kissed her very loud.

The Patent-Leather-Slipper-Child,
Was shocked at such a sight,
She only offered you her cheek
At morning and at night.

Oh, Half-Soled-Boots-With-Toecaps-Child
Her happy laughing face
Does like a scented summer rose
Make sweet the dullest place.

Oh, Patent-Leather-Slipper-child,
My dear I'm well content,

To have my daughter in my arms
And not an ornament.

A Joyful Song of Five!

Come, let us all sing very high
And all sing very loud –
And keep on singing in the street
Until there's quite a crowd.

And keep on singing in the house
And up and down the stairs
Then underneath the furniture
Let's all play Polar Bears

And crawl about with doormats on
And growl and howl and squeak
Then in the garden let us fly
And play at 'Hide and seek'

And 'Here We Gather Nuts and May'
'I Wrote a Letter,' too
'Here we go round the Mulberry Bush,'
'The Child Who Lost its Shoe'

And every game we *ever* played
And then – to stay alive –
Let's end with lots of Birthday cake
Because Today You're Five.

The Candle Fairy

The candle is a fairy house
That's smooth and round and white
And Mother carries it about
Whenever it is night.

Right at the top a fairy lives
A lovely yellow one
And if you blow a little bit
It has all sorts of fun.

It bows and dances by itself
In such a clever way

And then it stretches very tall
'Well, it grows fast' you say.

The little chimney of the house
Is black and really sweet
And there the candle fairy stands
Though you can't see its feet.

And when the dark is very big
And you've been having dreams
Then Mother brings the candle in
How friendly like it seems!

It's only just for Mothers that
The candle fairy comes
And if you play with it – it bites
Your fingers and your thumbs.

But still you love it very much
This candle fairy, dear
Because, at night, it always means
That Mother's very near.

The Last Thing

Now the Dustman's reached our door,
Now the blinds are all pulled down
Everything is growing quiet
Even noises in the town.

You, all ready for your bed,
First kneel down by Mummy's chair
Fold your hands upon her lap
Learn to say a little prayer.

First, just 'thank you, God' – and then
'Gentle Jesus meek and mild'
Last 'I lay me down to sleep
Make me please a better child.'

Very solemn, very grave.
Then you get up from your knees
And you rush to Daddy kins
'Now the Barley-sugar – please.'

A Quarrel

We stood in the veg'table garden
As angry and cross as could be
'Cause you said you would not 'beg pardin'
For eating my radish at tea.

I said 'I shall go and tell Mummy,
I *hope* that it's making you ill –
I *hope* you've a pain in your tummy
And then she will give you a pill.'

But you called out 'Goodbye then, for ever
Go and play with *your* silly old toys
If you think you're so grown up and clever
I'll run off and play with the Boys.'

A Song for Our Real Children

We sang 'Up In the Cherry Tree'
Both sittin' on the lawn
And then we sang 'The Busy Bee'
And 'Jesus Chris' was born.'

O dear, we had a lovely time
An' when the tea bell rang
All by ourselves we made a rhyme
To tell Nurse how we sang.

So when we both is old and wise
With babies six and seven
We'll say 'We made this for a s'prise
When you was all in Heaven.'

Grown Up Talks

Half-Past-Six and I were talking
In a very grown-up way
We had got so tired with running
That we did not want to play.

'How do babies come – I wonder'
He said – looking at the sky
'Does God mix the things together
And just make them – like a pie?'

I was really not quite certain,
But it sounded very nice
It was all that we could think of
And one book said 'sugar and spice.'

Half-past-six said – he's so clever –
Cleverer than me – I mean
'I suppose God makes the black ones
When the saucepan isn't clean!'

You won't understand this – 'cause you're a Boy

If you have never been a girl
You cannot know the sin
To wear just 'dress material'
To keep your 'bodies' in.

An' I shall never quite forget
The feeling that I felt
When Mummy went and bought for me
A Ladies Leather Belt.

The Lonesome Child

The baby in the looking glass,
Is smiling through at me;
She has her teaspoon in her hand,
Her feeder on for tea;

And if I look behind her, I
Can see the table spread.
I wonder if she has to eat
The nasty crusts of bread.

Her doll, like mine, is sitting close
Beside her special chair.
She has a pussy on her cup
It must be my cup there.

Her picture book is on the floor,
The cover's just the same,
And tidily upon the shelf
I see my ninepins game.

O baby in the looking glass,
Come through and play with me,

And if you will, I promise, dear,
To eat your crusts at tea.

Evening Song of the Thoughtful Child

Shadow children, thin and small,
Now the day is left behind,
You are dancing on the wall,
On the curtains, on the blind.

On the ceiling, children, too
Peeking round the nursery door,
Let me come and play with you,
As we always played before.

Let's pretend that we have wings
And can really truly fly
Over every sort of things
Up and up into the sky.

Where the sweet star children play,
It does seem a dreadful rule,
They must stay inside all day
I suppose they go to school.

And tonight, dears, do you see
They are having such a race
With their Father Moon – the tree
Almost hides his funny face.

Shadow children, once at night,
I was all tucked up in bed,
Father Moon came – such a fright!
Through the window poked his head.

I could see his staring eyes
O my dears – I was afraid
That was not a nice surprise
And the *dreadful* noise I made.

Let us make a Fairy Ring
Shadow children, hand in hand
And our songs quite softly sing
That we learned in Fairy land.

Shadow children, thin and small
See – the day is far behind

And I kiss you – on the wall
On the curtains – on the blind.

Autumn Song

Now's the time when children's noses
All become as red as roses
And the colour of their faces
Makes me think of orchard places.
Where the juicy apples grow
And tomatoes – in a row.

And today – the hardened sinner
Never could be late for dinner
But will jump up to the table
Just as soon as he is able.
Ask for three times hot roast mutton
Oh! the shocking little glutton.

Come then, find your ball and racquet,
Pop into your winter jacket,
With the lovely bear-skin lining,
While the sun is brightly shining,
Let us run and play together
And just *love* the Autumn Weather.

Collection Ends

'Out here it is the Summer time'

Out here it is the Summer time
The days are hot and white
The gardens are ablaze with flowers
The sky with stars at night.
And [?] past my [?] bed
I watch the sparkling bay – – –
With London ever calling me
The live long day.

The people all about our place
They're meaning to be kind
They drive around to visit me

From miles and miles behind.
But I had rather sit alone
Why can't they stay away.
It's London ever calling me
The live long day.

I know the bush is beautiful
The cities up to date
In life, they say, we're on the top
It's England, though, that's late.
But I, with all my longing heart,
I care not what they say
It's London ever calling me
The live long day.

When I get back to London streets
When I am there again
I shall forget that Summer's here
While I am in the rain.
But I shall only feel at last
The wizard has his way
And London's ever calling me
The live long day.

'London London I know what I shall do'

London London I know what I shall do.
I have been almost stifling here
And mad with love of you
And poverty I welcome, yes –

A Fairy Tale

Now this is the story of Olaf
Who, ages and ages ago,
Lived right on the top of a mountain
A mountain all covered with snow.

And he was quite pretty and tiny
With beautiful curling fair hair
And small hands like delicate flowers
Cheeks kissed by the cold mountain air.

He lived in a hut made of pine wood
Just one little room and a door
A table, a chair, and a bedstead
And animal skins on the floor.

Now Olaf was partly a fairy
And so never wanted to eat
He thought dewdrops and raindrops were plenty
And snowflakes – and all perfumes sweet.

In the daytime when sweeping and dusting
And cleaning were quite at an end
He would sit very still on the doorstep
And dream – O – that he had a friend.

Somebody to come when he called them
Somebody to catch by the hand
Somebody to sleep with at night time
Somebody who'd quite understand.

One night in the middle of winter
He lay wide awake on his bed
Outside there was fury of tempest
And calling of wolves to be fed.

Thin wolves, grey and silent as shadows
And Olaf was frightened to death
He had peeked through a crack in the doorpost
He had *seen* the white smoke of their breath.

But suddenly over the storm wind
He heard a small voice, pleadingly
Cry 'I am a snow fairy, Olaf
Unfasten the window for me.'

So he did, and there flew through the opening
The daintiest prettiest sprite
Her face and her dress and her stockings
Her hands and her curls – were all white.

And she said: 'O you poor little stranger
Before I am melted, you know,
I have brought you a valuable present
A little brown fiddle and bow.

So now you can never be lonely
With a fiddle, you see, for a friend
But all through the Summer and Winter
Play beautiful songs without end.'

And then, – O – she melted like water
But Olaf was happy at last
The fiddle he tucked in his shoulder
He held his small bow very fast . . .

So perhaps, on the quietest of evenings,
If you listen you may hear him soon
The child who is playing the fiddle
'Way up in the cold lonely moon.

Vignette

This is Angelica
Fallen from Heaven
Fallen from Heaven
Into my arms.

Will you go back again
Little Angelica
Back into Heaven
Out of my arms.

'No,' said Angelica
Here is my Heaven
Here is my heaven
Here in your arms

Not out of Heaven
But into my Heaven
Here have I fallen
Here in your arms.

In the Rangitaiki Valley

Oh, valley of waving broom
Oh, lovely, lovely light
Oh, heart of the world, red-gold!
Breast high in the blossom I stand
It beats about me like waves
Of a magical, golden sea

The barren heart of the world
Alive at the kiss of the sun
The yellow mantle of Summer

Flung over a laughing land
Warm with the warmth of her body
Sweet with the kiss of her breath

Oh, valley of waving broom
Oh, lovely, lovely light
Oh, mystical marriage of Earth
With the passionate Summer sun
To her lover she holds a cup
And the yellow wine o'erflows
He has lighted a little torch
And the whole of the world is ablaze
Prodigal wealth of love
Breast high in the blossom I stand

Youth

O Flower of Youth!
See in my hand I hold
This blossom flaming yellow and pale gold
And all its petals flutter at my feet
Can Death be sweet?

Look at it now!
Just the pale green is heart
Heart of the flower see is white and bare
The silken wrapping scattered on the ground
What have I found?

If one had come
On a sweet summer day
Breathless, half waking – full of youth I say
If one had come [. . .] from the glen
What happens then?

Sighing it dies
In the dawn flush of life
Never to know the terror and the strife
Which kills all summer blossoms when they blow.
Far better so
Ah! better better so.

1908

'Red as the wine of forgotten ages'

Red as the wine of forgotten ages
Yellow as gold by the sunbeams spun
Pink as the gowns of Aurora's pages
White as the robes of a sinless one
Sweeter than Araby's winds that blow
Roses. Roses I love you so.

The Grandmother

Underneath the cherry trees
The Grandmother in her lilac printed gown
Carried Little Brother in her arms.
A wind, no older than Little Brother,
Shook the branches of the cherry trees
So that the blossom snowed on her hair
And on her faded lilac gown
And all over Little Brother.
I said 'may I see?'
She bent down and lifted a corner of his shawl.
He was fast asleep.
But his mouth moved as if he were kissing.
'Beautiful,' said the Grandmother, nodding and smiling.
But my lips quivered,
And looking at her kind face
I wanted to be in the place of Little Brother
To put my arms round her neck
And kiss the two tears that shone in her eyes.

Butterflies

In the middle of our porridge plates
There was a blue butterfly painted
And each morning we tried who should reach the butterfly first.
Then the Grandmother said: 'Do not eat the poor butterfly.'
That made us laugh.
Always she said it and always it started us laughing.
It seemed such a sweet little joke.
I was certain that one fine morning
The butterfly would fly out of the plates
Laughing the teeniest laugh in the world
And perch on the Grandmother's cap.

Little Brother's Secret

When my birthday was coming
Little Brother had a secret
He kept it for days and days
And just hummed a little tune when I asked him.
But one night it rained
And I woke up and heard him crying.
Then he told me.
'I planted two lumps of sugar in your garden
Because you love it so frightfully
I thought there would be a whole sugar tree for your birthday
And now it will all be melted.'
O, the darling!

The Man with the Wooden Leg

There was a man lived quite near us
He had a wooden leg and a goldfinch in a green cage
His name was Farkey Anderson
And he'd been in a war to get his leg.
We were very sad about him
Because he had such a beautiful smile
And was such a big man to live in a very little house.
When he walked on the road his leg did not matter so much
But when he walked in his little house
It made an ugly noise.
Little Brother said his goldfinch sang the loudest of all other birds,

So that he should not hear his poor leg
And feel too sorry about it.

Little Brother's Story

We sat in front of the fire
Grandmother was in the rocking chair doing her knitting
And Little Brother and I were lying down flat.
'Please tell us a story, Grandmother,' we said
But she put her head on one side and began counting her stitches
'Suppose you tell me one instead.'
I made up one about a spotted tiger
That had a knot in his tail
But though I liked that about the knot
I didn't know why it was put there
So I said: 'Little Brother's turn.'
'I know a perfect story,' he cried, waving his hands.
Grandmother laid down her knitting.
'Do tell us, dear.'
'Once upon a time there was a bad little girl
And her mummy gave her the slipper – and that's all.'
It was not a very special story.
But we pretended to be very pleased
And Grandmother gave him jumps on her lap.

The Candle

By my bed, on a little round table
The Grandmother placed a candle.
She gave me three kisses telling me they were three dreams
And tucked me in just where I loved being tucked.
Then she went out of the room and the door was shut.
I lay still, waiting for my three dreams to talk
But they were silent.
Suddenly I remembered giving her three kisses back
Perhaps, by mistake, I had given my three little dreams.

I sat up in bed.
The room grew big – O bigger far than a church.
The wardrobe, quite by itself, as big as a house
And the jug on the washstand smiled at me.
It was not a friendly smile.

I looked at the basket chair where my clothes lay folded.
The chair gave a creak as though it were listening for something.
Perhaps it was coming alive and going to dress in my clothes.

But the awful thing was the window
I could not think what was outside.
No tree to be seen, I was sure,
No nice little plant or friendly pebbly path.
Why did she pull the blind down every night?
It was better to know.

I crunched my teeth and crept out of bed.
I peeped through a slit of the blind
There was nothing at all to be seen
But hundreds of friendly candles all over the sky
In remembrance of frightened children.
I went back to bed.
The three dreams started singing a little song.

When I was a Bird

I climbed up the karaka tree
Into a nest all made of leaves
But soft as feathers.
I made up a song that went on singing all by itself
And hadn't any words but got sad at the end.
There were daisies in the grass under the tree.
I said, just to try them:
'I'll bite off your heads and give them to my little children to eat.'
But they didn't believe I was a bird
They stayed quite open.
The sky was like a blue nest with white feathers
And the sun was the mother bird keeping it warm.
That's what my song said: though it hadn't any words.
Little Brother came up the path, wheeling his barrow
I made my dress into wings and kept very quiet
Then when he was quite near I said: 'sweet, sweet.'
For a moment he looked quite startled
Then he said: 'Pooh, you're not a bird; I can see your legs.'
But the daisies didn't really matter
And Little Brother didn't really matter;
I felt *just* like a bird.

Ave

Ah! never more again
Never more again
Cries my soul in pain
Elëanore.

– – – – –

Ah! never more again
Falls the winter rain
Where thy head is lain
Elëanore.

– – – – –

Ah! my life is dead with sorrow
Ah for me there is no morrow
Thou from me my life didst borrow
Elëanore.

– – – – –

All the world is dark and dreary
E'en the sea is very weary
And the wind is wild and eerie
Elëanore.

– – – – –

'Lo I am standing the test'

Lo I am standing the test.
Laughing I go to my doom
Crushed on the great Earth's breast
And the Night for Shroud and tomb.

I betwixt Heaven and Earth
I on the window sill
Sitting here shaken with mirth
For I have lived my fill.

These are the words that I write
Scribble and just let them lie
While I pass into the night,
Take a great leap and die.

Riding alone is the moon
Through the great black starlit space
I shall look like her quite soon
I with my dead white face.

Far far below the court
Search for me there O my friend
I – I shall not count for aught
Yet I alone choose my end.

Haunted by night and by day
By shadows that cry to me – flee
Loose the great bonds leave your place
Learn what Existence can be.

Why Love is Blind

The Cupid child, tired of the winter day,
Wept and lamented for the skies of blue.
Till, foolish child! he cried his eyes away –
And violets grew.

'Out to the glow of the sunset, brother'

Out to the glow of the sunset, brother
Come with me
The wild waves play and embrace one another
Let us join their play my brother
Far away out at sea.

The sky is wondrous fair O brother
(Let us go)
The great sad Ocean shall be our Mother
We are tired and she will rock us brother
Gently to and fro.

Why do you linger here, my brother
(The sunset dies)
The sun and the sea say goodbye to each other
Come away, soon will be too late, my brother
Hark to the sea birds' cries.

Ah! all the glory has faded brother
The sea is still
She is waiting for us to creep under the cover
Of her great blue wings O brother, brother
Peace, we shall soon be still.

We stood together on the shore
The wind was moaning, the sun was dying

And the sea was crying crying, crying
For ever more.

We knew we should part on the morrow
We looked towards the sea and sky
And dared not move, and could not cry
For sorrow.

We did not know when we should meet
We only knew we had to part.

In the Tropics

How I love to wake in the morning
And know I am far out at sea
That night has gone, day is dawning
And I am with thee, with thee.

And I go out on deck in the sunshine
And the sea is as calm as a lake
See the flying fish far on the starboard
There is no sound the silence to break.

Save the lazy flap-flap of the mainsail
And the voice of the men at their tasks –
O Sea, how I love to be with thee
'Tis all that my tired spirit asks.

And we pace the ship, forard in silence
Your hand clasped in mine, and our eyes
Gazing far on the distant horizon
To the place our future home lies.

And at night, when the stars come out slowly
And we glide ever on in the dark
And the phosphorus floods past like fireballs
There is no sound our silence to mark.

O the peace, and the hush, and the beauty
I would that my sea life would last
And I left all my Soul in the Tropics
And my heart 'tis bound up in the past.

'I am quite happy for you see'

I am quite happy for you see
My books and music stay with me
My days and nights are melody.

And in the morning the great sun
Climbs through the windows one by one
Calls to me, laughs that the day's begun.

Late in the night – when I lie awake
Comes the quiet and secret moon to make
Delicate lamplight for my sake.

And from my window – down below
There is a box where the Spring flowers grow
Daffodils golden breathe and blow.

To Pan

How we have spoken of Pan together
    Do you remember – long ago?
Fast bound in by the winter's weather
    Window bars even heaped with snow.

Prisoners we with our books beside us
    Emerson, Meredith, Borrow, the man
Chosen – of all our friends to guide us,
    Captain in chief of our caravan.

Do you remember our plans to wander
    To find the altar of Pan one day?
Over the hills and away back yonder
    Kneel in the heather. . . I think to pray?

Pan, great Pan! In the soul of his playing
    We – the lovers – were giants, we said,
Irresistible, unerring, slaying
    By heart's witchery. . . 'cut off his head'.

So we would laugh, your arm round my shoulder,
    Laugh at the world that was ours to keep,
Cry that we two could never grow older,
    We were awake though the world lay asleep.

Laugh until Pan . . . the munificent giver,
    Woke from a slumber to play his part,

Plucked a reed from the frozen river
        Fashioned the song of our firebound heart.

'Capable of a subjective passion,'
        So you stigmatise me, today –
Well, my dear, we pass in this fashion
        But Pan, God Pan, continues to play.

October (To V.M.B.)

Dim mist of a fog-bound day . . .
From the lilac trees that droop in St Mary's Square
The dead leaves fall, a silent, shivering, cloud.
Through the grey haze the carts loom heavy, gigantic
Down the dull street. Children at play in the gutter
Quarrel and cry; their voices sound flat and toneless.
With a sound like the shuffling tread of some giant monster
I hear the trains escape from the stations near, and *tear* their
        way into the country.
Everything looks fantastic, repellent. I see from my window
An old man pass, dull, formless, like the stump of a dead tree moving.
The virginia creeper, like blood, streams down the face of the houses.
Even the railings, blackened and sharply defined, look evil and
  strangely malignant.

Dim mist of a fog-bound day,
From the lilac trees that droop in St Mary's Square
The dead leaves fall, a silent, fluttering crowd.
Dead thoughts that, shivering, fall on the barren earth. . .
. . . Over and under it all the muttering murmur of London.

'You ask me for a picture of my room'

You ask me for a picture of my room.

And through the wood he lightly came
And lightly caught me by the hand
He called me by my childish name
How could I understand?

He led me by a secret way
A little path that seemed to wind
And lose itself – the shining day
Was very far behind.

For here the trees so thickly stood
The sunlight could not filter through
Dear Christ it was a magic wood
And magic boughs that grew.

And I have waited long for thee
He scorched me with his fiery breath.
I am the one eternity
Not – love – not love – but Death.

The very silence seemed to break
And quiver with a thousand things
The bird of passion seemed to wake
I felt it spread its wings

And fly from his head into mine
He led me to a little bower
All smothered with the creeping vine
And purple passion flower.

And there we kissed and passionately
We clung together – all the past
Blotted from out my memory
I knew I had found love at last.

Words for T.W.T.

And which do I love most my dear
The substance or the shadow.

A Sad Truth

We were so hungry, he and I
We knew not what to do
And so we bought a sugar cake
Oh, quite enough for two.

We ate it slowly, bit by bit
And not a crumb was wasted
It was the very best, we said
That we had ever tasted.

But all this happened years ago
Now we are rich and old

Yet we cannot buy such sugar cake
With our united gold.

A Song of Summer

At break of day the Summer sun
Shines through our windows one by one
He takes us by his great warm hand
And the world is changed to Fairyland.
He gives us fairy bread to eat
And fairy nectar, strange and sweet
While a magic bird the whole day long
Sings in our hearts his mating song.

The Winter Fire

Winter without, but in the curtained room
Flushed into beauty by a fluttering fire
Shuttered and blinded from the ugly street
A woman sits – her hands locked round her knees
And bending forward . . . O'er her loosened hair
The firelight spins a web of shining gold
Sears her pale mouth with kisses passionate
Wraps her tired body in a hot embrace.
Propped by the fender her rain-sodden boots
Steam, and suspended from the iron bed
Her coat and skirt – her wilted, draggled hat.
But she is happy, huddled by the fire
All recollections of the dingy day
Dwindle to nothingness, and she forgets
That in the street outside the rain which falls
Muddies the pavement to a greasy brown,
That in the morning she must start again
And search again for that which will not come.
She does not feel the sickening despair
That creeps into her bones throughout the day.
In her great eyes – dear Christ – the light of dreams
Lingered and shone. And she, a child again
Saw pictures in the fire. Those other days
The rambling house, the cool sweet-scented rooms
The portraits on the walls, and China bowls
Filled with 'pot pourri.' On her rocking chair

Her sofa pillow broidered with her name –
She saw again her bedroom, very bare
The blue quilt worked with daisies white and gold
Where she slept, dreamlessly . . .
. . . Opening her window, from the new-mown lawn
The fragrant, fragrant scent of perfumed grass
The lilac tossing in the shining air
Its purple plumes. The laurustinus bush
Its blossoms like pale hands among the leaves
Quivered and swayed. And, oh, the sun
That kisses her to life and warmth again
So she is young, and stretches out her arms . . .
The woman, huddled by the fire, restlessly stirs
Sighing a little, like a sleepy child
While the red ashes crumble into grey.

Suddenly, from the street, a burst of sound
A barrel organ turned and jarred and wheezed
The drunken, bestial, hiccoughing voice of London.

In the Church

In the church, with folded hands she sits
Watching the ivy beat upon the pane
Of a stained glass window, until she is fain
To shut her eyes – – – yet ever hears it tapping.

> 'Come out' says the ivy
> 'I spring from the mound
> Where your husband lies buried.
> You, too, in the ground
> (The hour is at hand)
> You must lie down beside him.'

In the church with folded hands she sits
Seeing a bride and bridegroom, hand in hand
Stand at the altar, but no wedding band
Crowns the young bride – save a chaplet of ivy leaves.

The Lilac Tree

The branches of the lilac tree
Are bent with blossom – in the air

They sway and languish dreamily
And we, pressed close, are kissing there
The blossoms falling on her hair –
Oh, lilac tree, Oh, lilac tree
Shelter us, cover us, secretly.

The branches of the lilac tree
All withered in the winter air
Shiver – a skeleton in minstrelsy[?]
Soon must the tree stand stripped and bare
And I shall never find her there
Oh, lilac tree, Oh, lilac tree
Shower down thy leaves and cover me.

On the Sea Shore

Deafening roar of the ocean
The wild waves thunder and beat
Sea weed, fragments of wreckage
They fling them up to her feet.

She, her pale face worn with waiting
Stands alone in the shuddering day
And watches the flight of a sea-gull
Wearily winging its way.

'Why do you scream, oh sea bird,
And why do you fly to me?'
'I am the soul of your lover
Who lies drowned far out at sea.'

Revelation

All through the Winter afternoon
We sat together, he and I . . .
Down in the garden every tree
Seemed frozen to the sky

Yes, every twisted tree that bared
Its naked limbs for sacrifice
Was patterned like a monstrous weed
Upon a lake of ice.

It was as though the pallid world
Was gripped in the embrace of Death.

He wrapt the garden in his shroud
He killed it with his breath.

So through the Winter afternoon
We sat together by the fire
And in its heart strange magic worlds
Would build, would flame, expire

In an intensity of flame –
Our books were heaped upon the floor
Fantastic chronicles of men
Of cities seen no more

Of countries buried by the sea
Of people who had laughed and cried
And madly suffered – who had held
The world – and then, had died.

A faded pageant of the past
Trooped by us in the gathering gloom
And we could hear strange, muffled cries
Like voices from the tomb.

And sometimes as we turned a page
We heard the shivering sound of rain
It trickled down the window glass
Like tears upon the pane.

We two, it seemed, were shut apart
Were fire bound from the Winter world
And all the secrets of the past
Lay, like a scroll unfurled.

As through the Winter afternoon
We dreaming, read of many lands
And woke . . . to find the Book of Life
Spread open in our hands.

The Trio

Out in the fog stained, mud stained street they stand
Two women and a man . . . Their draggled clothes
Hang on their withered bodies. It is cold
So cold the very rain and fog feel starved
And bite into their scarcely covered bones.
Their purple hands move restlessly, at first

They try to shield them with their thread-bare cuffs
Then thrust them in their coats, and then again
Blow on their fingers, but to no avail.
The women wear a strangely faded look
As though the rain which beat upon them both
And, never ceasing, always dripping down
Had worn away their features . . . In their eyes
Hunger had lit a pallid, wavering torch . . .
The man is like a seedy, draggled bird
He frowns upon the women, savagely . . .
Opposite them a warehouse, huge and grey
And ugly – in the ghostly light of fog
It looms gigantic – through the open doors
Men and more men are passing out and in.
. . . Then, at a signal from the draggled man
The women sing – God, from their withered mouths
A tragedy of singing issues forth
High pitched and wandering, crazy tuneless tune
Over and over comes the same refrain
'Say, shepherds, have you seen my Flora pass this way. . .'
The simple words hang trembling in the air
So strange, so foreign, if the filthy street
Had blossomed into daisies; if a vine
Had wreathed itself upon the warehouse wall
It would have been more natural – they sing
Shivering, staring – on their withered mouths
The winter day has set a frozen kiss . . .
Coldly impassive, cynically grim
The warehouse seems to sneer at them and cry
'My doors are shut and bolted, locked and barred
And in my bosom nurture I my spawn
Upon the blackened blood of my stone heart
I blind their eyes. I stop their mouths with dust
I hypnotise them with the chink of gold
They search and grope – but ever out of reach
I keep it, jingling. They can never hear
Your Floras and your shepherds . . .' Through the fog
The quavering voices fall and rise again . . .
Are silent – and the trio shuffles on.

1909

The Arabian Shawl

'It is cold outside, you will need a coat –
What! this old Arabian shawl!
Bind it about your head and throat,
These steps . . . it is dark . . . my hand . . . you might fall.'

What has happened? What strange, sweet charm
Lingers about the Arabian shawl . . .
Do not tremble so! There can be no harm
In just remembering – that is all.

'I love you so – I will be your wife,'
Here, in the dark of the Terrace wall,
Say it again. Let that other life
Fold us like the Arabian shawl.

'Do you remember?' . . . 'I quite forget,
Some childish foolishness, that is all,
To-night is the first time we have met . . .
Let me take off my Arabian shawl!'

Sleeping Together

Sleeping together . . . how tired you were! . . .
How warm our room . . . how the firelight spread
On walls and ceiling and great white bed!
We spoke in whispers as children do,
And now it was I – and then it was you
Slept a moment, to wake – 'My dear,
I'm not at all sleepy,' one of us said. . . .

Was it a thousand years ago?
I woke in your arms – you were sound asleep –

And heard the pattering sound of sheep.
Softly I slipped to the floor and crept
To the curtained window, then, while you slept,
I watched the sheep pass by in the snow.

O flock of thoughts with their shepherd Fear
Shivering, desolate, out in the cold,
That entered into my heart to fold!
A thousand years . . . was it yesterday
When we, two children of far away,
Clinging close in the darkness, lay
Sleeping together? . . . How tired you were! . . .

The Quarrel (2)

Our quarrel seemed a giant thing,
It made the room feel mean and small,
The books, the lamp, the furniture,
The very pictures on the wall –

Crowded upon us as we sat
Pale and terrified, face to face.
'Why do you stay?' she said, 'my room
Can never be your resting place.'

'Katinka, ere we part for life,
I pray you walk once more with me.'
So down the dark, familiar road
We paced together, silently.

The sky – it seemed on fire with stars!
I said: – 'Katinka dear, look up!'
Like thirsty children, both of us
Drank from that giant loving cup.

'Who were those *dolls*?' Katinka said
'What were their stupid, vague alarms?'
And suddenly we turned and laughed
And rushed into each other's arms.

Spring Wind in London

I blow across the stagnant world
I blow across the sea,

For me the sailor's flag unfurled
For me the uprooted tree.
My challenge to the world is hurled;
The world must bow to me.

I drive the clouds across the sky,
I huddle them, like sheep;
Hercules' shepherd's dog am I
And shepherd's watch I keep
If in the quiet vales they lie
I blow them up the steep.

And when a little child is ill
I pause, and with my hand
I wave the window curtain frill
That he may understand
Outside the wind is blowing still
It is a pleasant land.

Lo! In the tree-tops do I hide,
In every living thing;
On the moon's yellow wings I glide,
In the wild rose I swing;
On the sea-horse's back I ride,
And what then do I bring?

Oh, stranger in a foreign place
See what I bring to you
This rain – like tears upon your face
I tell you – tell you true
I came from that forgotten place
Where once the heather grew.

All the wild sweetness of the flower
Tangled against a wall,
It was that magic, silent hour;
The branches grew so tall
They twined themselves into a bower;
The sun shone – and the fall

Of yellow blossom in the grass
You feel that golden rain?
Both of you tried to hold, alas.
Both could not hold – in vain.
A memory, stranger, so I pass
I will not come again.

'I could find no rest'

I could find no rest
Tossed and turned, and cried aloud, I suffer.
In my tortured breast
Turned the knife, and probed the flesh more deeply.

Up against it – Life seemed like a wall
Brick and fouled and grimed.

Oh delicate branches reaching out for the sun
The plants – on tiptoe stretching up [to] the light.

*

Do you see him?

Look, in the half light here,
High behind the curtain hanging there
See how it swings and trembles
Oh woman do not cry upon him so
It is the wind that makes the curtain blow
Pillow thy head upon my barren breast.
The child! he comes and stands beside my chair
Then claps his hands upon my eyes – 'who's there
Motherling.' 'I've no notion[?] – it's not *you*.'

The child he came into this room tonight
Groping his way – Why haven't you a light
Mother. My eyes were tired with weeping dear
I'm not afraid of dark if you stay here
(Oh the thought in heart and brain
He cannot see the light again.)

The child – he came and stood beside my chair
Then pressed his hands before my eyes. 'Who's there
Motherling – guess.' It never could be you.
Oh no – three guesses – wait then that's too few – – –
The only hands to bring her calm
Folded closely, palm to palm.

The child – he shyly stood in front of me
Am I too big to sit upon your knee
Motherling? I'm too tired for any fun
If I'm too heavy – 'No my little son.'
(The blood within her veins ran cold
Light he was – so light to hold)

The child – he hid his face against my breast
Crying 'Oh Mother let me rest.'

Floryan nachdenklich

Floryan sits in the black chintz chair,
An Indian curtain behind his head
Blue and brown and white and red.
Floryan sits quite still – quite still.
There is a noise like a rising tide
Of wind and rain in the black outside.
But the firelight leaps on Floryan's wall
And the Indian curtain suddenly seems
To stir and shake like a thousand dreams.
The Indian flowers drink the fire
As though it were sun, and the Indian leaves
Patter and sway to an echo breeze.
On the great brown boughs of the Indian tree
Little birds sing and preen their wings.
They flash through the sun like jewel rings.
And the great tree grows and moves and spreads
Through the silent room, and the rising tide
Of wind and rain on the black outside
Fades – and Floryan suddenly stirs
And lifts his eyes, and weeps to see
The dreaming flowers of the Indian tree.

To Stanislaw Wyspianski

From the other side of the world,
From a little island cradled in the giant sea bosom,
From a little land with no history,
(Making its own history, slowly and clumsily
Piecing together this and that, finding the pattern, solving the problem,
Like a child with a box of bricks),
I, a woman, with the taint of the pioneer in my blood,
Full of a youthful strength that wars with itself and is lawless,
I sing your praises, magnificent warrior; I proclaim your triumphant
    battle.
My people have had nought to contend with;
They have worked in the broad light of day and handled the clay with
    rude fingers

Life – a thing of blood and muscle; Death – a shovelling underground
of waste material.
What would they know of ghosts and unseen presences,
Of shadows that blot out reality, of darkness that stultifies morn?
Fine and sweet the water that runs from their mountains;
How could they know of poisonous weed, of rotted and clogging
tendrils?
And the tapestry woven from dreams of your tragic childhood
They would tear in their stupid hands,
The sad, pale light of your soul blow out with their childish laughter.
But the dead – the old – Oh Master, we belong to you there;
Oh Master, there we are children and awed by the strength of a giant;
How alive you leapt into the grave and wrestled with Death
And found in the veins of Death the red blood flowing
And raised Death up in your arms and showed him to all the people.
Yours a more personal labor than the Nazarene's miracles,
Yours a more forceful encounter than the Nazarene's gentle
commands.
Stanislaw Wyspianski – Oh man with the name of a fighter,
Across these thousands of sea-shattered miles we cry and proclaim you;
We say 'He is lying in Poland, and Poland thinks he is dead;
But he gave the denial to Death – he is lying there, wakeful;
The blood in his giant heart pulls red through his veins.'

Song of Karen the Dancing Child

(O little white feet of mine)
Out in the storm and the rain you fly
(Red red shoe the colour of wine)
Can the *children* hear my cry?

(O little white feet of mine)
Never a child in the whole great town
(Red red shoes the colour of wine)
Lights out and the blinds pulled down.

(O little white feet of mine)
Never a light on a window pane,
(Red red shoes the colour of wine)
And the wild wet cry of the rain.

(O little white feet of mine)
Shall I *never* again be still?
(Red red shoes the colour of wine)
And away over valley and hill.

(O little white feet of mine)
Children – children, open the door!
(Red red shoes the colour of wine)
And the wind shrieks 'never more.'

Loneliness

Now it is Loneliness who comes at night
Instead of Sleep, to sit beside my bed.
Like a tired child I lie and wait her tread,
I watch her softly blowing out the light.
Motionless sitting, neither left nor right

She turns, and weary, weary droops her head.
She, too, is old; she, too, has fought the fight.
So! with the laurel she is garlanded.

Through the sad dark the slowly ebbing tide
Breaks on a barren shore, unsatisfied.
A strange wind flows . . . then silence. I am fain
To turn to Loneliness, to take her hand,
Cling to her, waiting, till the barren land
Fills with the dreadful monotone of rain.

The Sea-Child

Into the world you sent her, mother,
   Fashioned her body of coral and foam,
Combed a wave in her hair's warm smother,
   And drove her away from home.

In the dark of the night she crept to the town
   And under a doorway she laid her down,
The little blue child in the foam-fringed gown.

And never a sister and never a brother
   To hear her call, to answer her cry.
Her face shone out from her hair's warm smother
   Like a moonkin up in the sky.

She sold her corals; she sold her foam;
   Her rainbow heart like a singing shell
Broke in her body: she crept back home.

Peace, go back to the world, my daughter,
   Daughter, go back to the darkling land;
There is nothing here but sad sea water,
   And a handful of sifting sand.

Sea Song

I will think no more of the sea!
Of the big green waves
And the hollowed shore,
Of the brown rock caves
No more, no more
Of the swell and the weed
And the bubbling foam.

Memory dwells in my far away home,
She is nothing to do with me.

She is old and bent
With a pack
On her back.
Her tears all spent,
Her voice, just a crack.
With an old thorn stick
She hobbles along,
And a crazy song
Now slow, now quick,
Wheeks in her throat.

And every day
While there's light on the shore
She searches for something
Her withered claw
Tumbles the seaweed;
She pokes in each shell
Groping and mumbling
Until the night
Deepens and darkens,
And covers her quite,
And bids her be silent,
And bids her be still.

The ghostly feet
Of the whispery waves
Tiptoe beside her.
They follow, follow
To the rocky caves
In the white beach hollow . . .
She hugs her hands,
She sobs, she shrills,
And the echoes shriek
In the rocky hills.
She moans: it is lost!
Let it be! Let it be!
I am old. I'm too cold
I am frightened . . . the sea
Is too loud . . . it is lost,
It is gone . . . . Memory
Wails in my far away home.

'A gipsy's camp was in the copse'

A gipsy's camp was in the copse
Three felted tents with beehive tops
And round black marks where fires had been
And one old wagon painted green
And three ribbed horses wrenching grass
And three wild boys to watch me pass
And one old woman by the fire
Hulking a rabbit warm from wire.

Collection: *The Earth Child*

DEDICATION:

'I nest in the tree of your soul
Without me you are dark and silent
Without you I homelessly wander'.

I

It has rained all day.
A tree grows outside my window
Heavily droop the boughs
The leaves smother closely
As though to protect the frail tree body
Mournfully swaying in the quiet air . . .
A grey bird alights on a branch
And lifts her throat and sings in the sighing tree.
O branch and bough and dusky, smothering leaves
Have you forgotten your summer fragrance?
Do you remember the time when you shook your blossom
Into the living air. . . . . laughing and trembling?
The grey bird does not forget: She holds your secret
And sings in her little wild heart to your mournful swaying

II

In the very early morning
Long before Dawn time
I lay down in the paddock

And listened to the cold song of the grass.
Between my fingers the green blades
And the green blades pressed against my body.
'Who is she leaning so heavily upon me?'
Sang the grass.
'Why does she weep on my bosom,
Mingling her tears with the tears of mystic lover?
Foolish little earth child!
It is not yet time
One day I shall open my bosom
And you shall slip in – but not weeping.
Then in the early morning
Long before Dawn time
Your lover will lie in the paddock.
Between his fingers the green blades
And the green blades pressed against his body . .
My song shall not sound cold to him
In my deep wave he will find the wave of your hair
In my strong sweet perfume, the perfume of your kisses.
Long and long he will lie there . .
Laughing – not weeping'.

III

Through the dark forest we walked apart and silently
Only the dead leaves beneath our feet kept up a ghostly conversation.
As we touched them – they cried out: 'It is all over you are killing us'.
Yet with swift steps and joyfully, we walked through the muffled forest.
A wild scent burst from the ground and broke over us in waves
The naked branches stiffened against the black air.
Behind us an army of ghosts mimicked our steps
They caught at the trailing shadows and fashioned them into cloaks.
And pretended that under their cloaks, like us, they were trembling and
    burning.
On the brow of the hill we stopped – the ghosts forsook us
The forest drew back and the road slipped into the plains.
A moon swung into the sky – we faced each other . .
He said! 'Do not fly away'.
I said: 'Are you a dream' . .
We touched each other's hands.

IV

The Sea called – I lay on the rocks and said;
'I am come'.
She mocked and showed her teeth
Stretching out her long green arms.
'Go away', she thundered.
'Then tell me what I am to do', I begged,
'If I leave you, you will not be silent
But cry my name in the cities
And wistfully entreat me in the plains and forests
All else I forsake to come to you – what must I do?'
'Never have I uttered your name' snarled the Sea
'There is no more of me in your body
Than the little salt tears you are frightened of shedding.
What can you know of my love on your brown rock pillow . .
Come closer'.

V

In an opal dream cave I found a fairy
Her wings were frailer than flower petals
Frailer far than snow flakes.
She was not frightened, but poised on my finger
Then delicately walked into my hand.
I shut the two palms of my hands together
And held her prisoner.
I carried her out of the opal cave
Then opened my hands.
First she became thistledown
Then a mote in a sunbeam
Then – nothing at all . .
Empty now is my opal dream cave.

VI

The fields are snowbound no longer
There are little blue lakes and flags of tenderest green.
The snow has been caught up into the sky
So many white clouds – and the blue of the sky is cold.
Now the sun walks in the forest
He touches the boughs and stems with his golden fingers

They shiver, and wake from slumber.
Over the barren branches he shakes his yellow curls.
. . Yet is the forest full of the sound of tears. .
A wind dances over the fields
Shrill and clear the sound of her waking laughter
Yet the little blue lakes tremble
And the flags of tenderest green bend and quiver.

VII

My belovèd rose out of the river
Her body was fashioned of moonlight
Shining weed was her hair.
She clung with both hands to my boat
Laughing and mocking. .
As for me I sat silently weeping
I was afraid of the river. .
She flung in my face a lily with five, white petals
But the heart of the water flower
Was choked with the river sand.
. . Mocking and laughing
My belovèd rose out of the river.

VIII

The tassels of the broom swept the long hillside
The fern trees built in the blue air
Their canopy of silver and green.
Little Brother lay with his head in my lap
Tired and happy.
I knew he was happy – yet I asked:
'Are you happy Little Brother?'
Then he sat up and shook back his hair
Laughing at my silly question . .
The gold of the broom is fairy treasure
And the fern trees have built a magic house.
I wish I were your fairy sister
I would make you live with me on this green hillside
And long for nothing else, Little Brother.

IX

In a narrow path of a wood I met a witch
She had a bag over her shoulder; she was gathering pine needles
I questioned: 'For what could you need so many needles?'
'Hng, hng', laughed the witch, 'Under the tallest tree in the world
My hundred sisters and I are stitching a garment
Big as the world and small as a baby's thimble.
It is woven from that which grows in the hidden places
It is frilled with the Ocean and bound with the poison weed.
We stitch and stitch but the garment never is finished
If it were you would not be asking
'Hie, hie', laughed the witch.

X

When my plant grew too big for the flowerpot
I carried it into the garden
I buried it deep in the mould.
Now it grows strongly among the other flowers. .
I can hardly distinguish between them
But there is an empty space in my room
And broken pieces strewn over the flower beds

XI

The door of your room is never opened.
Some times I stand before it, on tip toe, like a child
And wonder. 'Shall I knock?'
But my wise heart answers: 'No,
Perhaps he is working'.
Sometimes when my room is flooded with blue light
– The blue light that you love –
And I look out over the snow –
I wonder: 'Shall I call to him?'
But my wise heart answers: 'No,
Perhaps he is sleeping'.
Sometimes, still as a mouse
I crouch on the floor, finger on lip
And lean my head against the door panel
Trying to hear your pen move
Or the quick rustle of book leaves

In vain – my sad heart ventures:
'Perhaps he has gone away'.

XII

Across the red sky two birds flying
Plying with drooping wings
Silent and solitary, their ominous flight . .
All day the triumphant sun with yellow banners
Wooed and warred with the earth and when she yielded
Stabbed her heart; Gathered her blood in a chalice
Spilling it over the evening sky –
Where the dark plumaged birds go flying, flying.
Quiet the earth lies, wrapt in her mournful shadow
Her sightless eyes turned to the evening sky
And the restlessly seeking birds.

XIII

I ran to the forest for shelter
Breathless, half sobbing
I put my arms round a tree.
'Protect me', I said, 'I am a lost child'.
But the tree showered silver drops on my face and hair.
A wind sprang up from the ends of the earth
It lashed the forest together
A huge green wave thundered and burst over my head.
'I pray you,' I implored 'Take care of me'.
But the wind snatched at my cloak and tugged at my tumbled hair.
Little rivers tore up the ground – swamping the bushes.
A frenzy possessed the earth: I felt that the earth was drowning
In a bubbling cavern of space, I alone
Smaller than the smallest fly was alive and terrified.
Then – for what reason I know not – I grew triumphant
'Well, kill me', I cried, and ran out into the Open.
But the storm ceased: The sun spread his wings
And floated serene on the silver pool of the sky
I put my hands over my face: I was blushing
But the trees swung together and delicately laughed.

XIV

A little wind crept round the house
It rattled the windows and door handles
'Let me in – let me in', it lamented.
But I pulled the curtain and lighted my lamp.
'O, how can you be so cruel', sobbed the wind
'My wings are tired: I want to go to sleep in your arms
There is peace in your heart, and a soft place for a tired child'.
I bent low over my books
'The night is so dark and the shadows are hurting me'.
I opened my window, leaned out and took the wind to my bosom
For a moment he lay silent
Then drew a long breath and opened his eyes
Maliciously smiling.
He sprang from my arms – blew out the lamp
Scattered the book leaves, leapt and danced on the floor
'Did you know', he sang,
'There was a spark in your heart
I have kindled it into flame with my breath –
Now rest if you can'.

XV

Why are you smiling so?
Girl face in the shadow
Your open brow, your smoothly banded hair
The painful shadow under your eyes,
These do not speak of joy –
Yet your mouth is tremulously smiling,
Is it a dream that makes you so happy?
Have you been promised a lover?
Has the Dawn given you a flowering branch?
Answer me in your dream speech
Girl face in the shadow
I shall quite understand and keep your secret.
'I smile', said the girl face in the shadow,
'Because I lie asleep on the quiet heart of Oblivion –
With no dreams at all and no treacherous promises,
And because I know that never any more
Shall I see the flowers of the night sky
Plucked by the cold hand of Dawn'.

XVI

From a far distant land
My friend is coming to me,
To-day or to-morrow I shall see the white sails of his boat
And the gay flags of greeting
Blowing out in the wind
Under the weight of such treasure
The sea moves restlessly
Each shy wave is crowned with magic blossom
Each rainbow shell sings of the melody of his voice.
Alone on the desolate strand I keep my vigil
I have built a fire of dried boughs and scented heather
Come quickly from the far distant land
My friend and brother –
The fire burns low
Let us break up your ship and cast it on to the burning
So that you may never go sailing any more.

XVII

You put your hands behind your back
'Which one will you have?' – you said
We laughed like happy children.
'The right', I said –
But your right hand was empty.
'Then the left'.
That too, held nothing at all –
I put my hands behind my back –
'It is your turn to choose'.
'Both', you said, gravely.
I stretched out my empty hands.
You laughed and held them against your face.
We were playing a childish game no longer.
Our gift was too big for one pair of hands to hold,
Could my hands span the world?
Yet I gave you the world.
Could your hands sound the depths of the sea?
Yet you gave me the sea.
If we joined hands, the miracle was so simple,
But apart it was quite impossible.

XVIII

There are days when the longing for you
Floods my heart – my veins are full of tears,
My hair seems to hold something of your wild scent,
I fancy my voice becomes as your voice,
And my slightest gesture shows my dependence on you.
There are days – O, they are many – when I am possessed by you.
Their shape and colour and sound – above all sound
(The voice of rain and wind
Leaves in a tree – the lapping of water,
The noise of cart wheels on a wet road
The barking of a dog heard from miles away
Children running softly on light feet –
A builder building a house and whistling as he works –)
All these simple things sink into the deep storm sea of my being
Where you are drowned and yet live – –
Yes, secretly, and in the deep water you cry to me.
'You who are born of me, to me you return
Did you fancy yourself a woman? – I know you a child
You were a child when you drowned me in this deep well,
Crying 'I have rid myself of a bogey – now I am free
But instead – O youngest of my children
You keep me within yourself . . . until the tide shall rise
The woman will be drowned and the child return to me
Through the dark water. The storm sea
That beats about the island where you were born'.

XIX

Night came – I opened my eyes
Outside the land was dark and dark the flowing river.
There were no stars to measure the sky vault
No pale moon floating on her cloud pillow.
It was all dark.
I walked abroad and lifted my head:
'If I choose I can stretch out my arms and dance over the whole world.
Not a hand can pluck at my sleeve, nobody can call after me
Nobody can find me'.
Through the long grass, I ran with naked feet
I plunged breast high among the bracken
I lost my way among the forest trees.
'Listen! The leaves are falling – they are falling all over me

Do you want to bury me under your leaves – then I am content'.
'No, dear child, we are decking you out in your holiday gown'.
I found a little cave powdered thickly with moss
I curled up inside it, pretending it was my home.
'O my hands and my feet have regained their power
They tell me just what it is they are touching, and that it is good'.
I wanted to sing a triumphant song that the war was over.
But my joy was too great – I smiled, shaking the tears from my eyes.
A little breeze, half scent, half mist, flew among the forest
It pulled the branch at the door of my cave . .
I lifted the branch and it floated in
We played a game without any words, like two shy children . .
Suddenly it shivered and flew away.
That frightened me
I left my green home and wandered deeper into the forest
I found a pool set about with sweet bushes.
From the cup of my hands I drank some of the water
Bitter and warm to taste – like the blood of the earth.
'Now, I can never go back!'
But the trees sang:
'Listen, a stranger is among us, Listen, a robber is hunting our paths,
Light! Protect us!'
Dawn fastened the sky with his great red hands
And the battle began again.

XX

There was a child once.
He came to play in my garden
He was quite pale and silent.
Only when he smiled I knew everything about him
I knew what he held in his pockets
And I knew the feel of his hands in my hands
And the most intimate tones of his voice
I led him down each secret path
Showing him the hiding place of all my treasures
I let him play with them, every one,
I put my singing thoughts in a little silver cage
And gave them to him to keep. . .
It was very dark in the garden
But never dark enough for us
On tip toe we walked among the deepest shades
We bathed in the shadow pools beneath the trees

Pretending we were under the sea
Once – near the boundary of the garden
We heard steps passing along the World-road
O how frightened we were!
I whispered 'Have you ever walked along that road?'
He nodded, and we shook the tears from our eyes . . .
There was a child once
He came – quite alone – to play in my garden
He was pale and silent
When we met we kissed each other
But when he went away, we did not even wave.

XXI

A jar of daffodils stood on the piano
In the half light, the leaves were thickly green
And the blossoms faintly luminous.
I leant over the piano and put my arms round the flower bowl
'Please play', I said.   ..   ..
The flowers quivered and shone
The leaves evermore thickly green pushed up
Until they smothered the ceiling and the flowers were set in them like a
    pattern
Then there was no ceiling, but the floor of the sky
Spilt over with gold.
The moon lay on the green floor
Her face shrouded in an opal veil
'Why are your wings folded?' I asked.
'Hush', answered the moon, 'Some one is playing'
Be quiet! A child of mine is crying for me.
Her tears are falling into the smallest flower cups
But her heart is so sad, she fancies she is quenching the fire of the
    stars.

XXII

In the swiftly moving sleigh
We sat curled up under the bear skin rugs
And talked of the dangers of life
The afternoon froze into a twilight, profounder than night
The trees in the forest, through which we passed,
Were patterned like monstrous weeds on a lake of ice . .

You told me all your adventures
And though they were very terrible and violent
I could not help laughing, sometimes you ceased speaking
Turned to me with a funny gravity
'I just escaped being killed'.
Then our laughter rang over the snow
I told you of three wrecks I had been in
Of a fire – and the time I was all-but-drowned in a river . .
Ever faster galloped the horses
The moon rose, touching the fantastic land with her silver fingers
How eloquently we described our adventures!
But it was useless.
They flew into space on the wings of our laughter . .
Curled up under the bear skin rugs.
We drove – it seemed – through the foam that breaks over the world
    edge.
On the one great adventure
That held us in silence and gravity.

XXIII

Round me in a ring
Finger on lip and sweetly silent
My shadow children.
We smile at one another
Then they stretch out their hands and pluck at my gown
'It is our turn to play.
The shortest little hour of the day is here – the hour before bedtime'.
I shake my head at them like a happy distracted mother
'You are really almost too old . .'
But with glad cries they fling themselves upon me
'. . What have you got for me in your pocket . .'
'. . Let me have the flower you are wearing . .'
'. . I shall take down your hair and turn you into a little girl . .'
'. . What have you been doing without us . .'
'. . Tell me about "A long – time – ago" . .'
Their hands, their hair, their flower faces,
I cover with kisses.
Through the dusk of the very shortest hour
We play our magic games.
Then in obedience, they slip away.
Only the very youngest shadow of all is loathe to go
He lies pillowed on my heart

Quiet, and so faintly breathing
That I am almost afraid.

XXIV

How quiet the Grandmother's hands
Folded in her lap,
In the lap of her dark gown
Her hands – faintly shining.
The firelight touches her silver hair
All else is in shadow.
Tenderly I watch her.
Are your thoughts folded so, little Grandmother
In the dark lap of the world
Are they faintly shining? . . .
I think your hands are asleep
They lie so still.
I think they are tilling over
In most secret sleep
The gifts they have held
And the kisses enfolded.
No, I am not weeping
And if my tears fall on your hands
It is but dew from my eyes
That opened under your smile.

XXV

In the purple heather
We lay like two gods on sun-flushed cloud pillows.
We could not see each other – so deep and thick our beds,
And therefore we talked heart-to-heart, like lovers on a night journey.
A pleasant, warm sweetness curled up in my hair.
And now, it seemed, we floated on a green river
That bore us high above the dark rocks of the world
Above those horrible caverns where we lost our way and were prisoned.
Serene delight floated through the green and purple waves
Our words took wings and flew like birds above us.
We did not demand or protest. They were very small birds
And shy – glad to find resting place
In the warm nests from which they sprang,
Yours into my heart, and mine into yours . . .

We were floating towards some ineffable Birth land
Where Peace – our new Mother, sat on the shore
Weaving the radiant sails of her boat
That would bring us home again.

XXVI

THE CHILD:

        How far have you come
        (O little cloud, heavy with rain)
        Where did you gather these tears
        That you weep so sadly?

THE CLOUD:

        From the creek where you washed your dolls' clothes
        From the pool where you sailed your paper boats.

THE CHILD:

        That was much too far
        (O little cloud heavy with rain)
        For such a small thing to travel
        Why did you come?

THE CLOUD:

        Your dolls are all battered and broken
        And your paper boats have blown away.

THE CHILD:

        But supposing I bought a new doll
        (O little cloud heavy with rain)
        And a most expensive sailing boat
        What should I do then?

THE CLOUD:

        The creek and the pool have disappeared
        You must play your game by the Big Sea.

XXVII

In the savage heart of the bush
The tui lifts her white throat
Three bell-like notes – then the answer she knows so well

And sings for herself – the love answer of laughter.
Her children – wreathed with the green garlands of sorrow
Answer her call.
They troop from the valleys and plains
From the stupid cities they never have fashioned
From the wharves where the strangers' ships find mooring.
From the green isles they pass in procession,
They kneel at altars white with clematis flower,
At brackish pools they drink their sacrament.
Now they are like giants walking
And their gestures are like the swaying movements of trees
The men call 'h a e re mai'
And the women answer with the love answer of laughter –
O bird of the bush, Spread your wings
And shelter your dusky children!

XXVIII

I had company tonight.
An old woman – some chrysanthemum flower – and a little child
We greeted each other politely.
Then the old woman took the rocking chair
The chrysanthemum shook out her petals
And the child lay on the floor, 'baking his bones'!
We said the days were growing very short
And the nights very cold –
But in the sun it was still warm.
'Warm as warm', laughed the child, kissing the chrysanthemum flower.
The old woman and I nodded and smiled.
By and bye we had supper –
Milk for the child from his special cup
But the chrysanthemum preferred water in a blue china bowl.
And we grew so festive and gay that the rain outside
Sounded like dance music; the wild wind
Swept round the house like a friendly watch-dog. .
To the child the chrysanthemum flower
Gave a little of her most delicious perfume.
He laughed with joy like any Spring baby
And his eyes shone like wood hyacinths.

To God the Father

To the little, pitiful God I make my prayer
The God with the long grey beard
And flowing robe fastened with a hempen girdle
Who sits nodding and muttering in the all-too-big throne of Heaven
What a long, long time, dear God, since you set the stars in their
    places
Girded the earth with the sea, and invented the day and night.
And longer the time since you looked through the blue window of
    Heaven
To see your children at play in a garden . . . . .
Now we are all stronger than you and wiser and more arrogant
In swift procession we pass you by.
'Who is that marionette nodding and muttering
In the all-too-big throne of Heaven?
Come down from your place, Grey Beard,
We have had enough of your play-acting!'
It is centuries since I believed in you
But today my need of you has come back.
I want no rose-coloured future
No books of learning – no protestations and denials –
I am sick of this ugly scramble,
I am tired of being pulled about –
O God, I want to sit on her knees
In the all-too-big throne of Heaven.
And fall asleep with my hands tangled in your grey beard.

Yesterday in Autumn

When you spoke of 'yesterday' you smiled
Half closing your eyes – you shook from your brow
The beating wings of your dreams
But tenderly.
Their caress as delicate as the wings of white butterflies.
You breathed slowly the memory of some enchanting perfume . . .
(We were crouched in front of the fire.
My hands full of chrysanthemum flower:
I sat biting the tattered petals).

'Yesterday' . . . so you whispered the name of your lover
Her kisses pressed that sweetness into your face
Her laughter thrilled your throat as you spoke her name . . .

A silent third – she crept between us,
Tentatively took your hand and stroked it . . .
I saw your fingers stir and the palm of your hand turn outwards.

She was the only reality in the room.
With parted lips I watched her draw more closely.

'Yesterday' . . . . .

Grave and cold I stared at the autumn flowers in my hands.

Then threw them on to the flames . . . . . . shivering.

Violets

The room is full of violets –
And yet there's but this little bowl
Of blossoms on the mantel-piece.

You stood beside them – ran your hands
Through the grey leaves – then bent your head
Over the flowers and breathless colour.

And elfishly you pulled the stems
All damp and shining, through your fingers
. . . Decorated our Tête de mort.

Splendid he looks with violets
Round his brow in a mazy tangle
A bud and a leaf behind one ear.

But if we admire him any longer
(It's close on midnight: time you went home)
I'm afraid he will burst into Mendelssohn's Spring Song

Boo – Bam – Boo! What an awful thought!
Quite dead drunk is our Tête de mort
In a room so full of violets.

Jangling Memory

Heavens above! Here's an old tie of yours
– Sea green dragons stamped on a golden ground
Ha! Ha! Ha! What children we were in those days.

Do you love me enough to wear it now –
Have you the courage of your pristine glories?
Ha! Ha! Ha! You laugh and shrug your shoulders.

Those were the days when a new tie spelt a fortune
We wore it in turn – I flaunted it as a waist belt.
Ha! Ha! Ha! What easily satisfied babies.

I think I'll turn it into a piano duster,
Give it to me, I'll polish my slippers on it!
Ha! Ha! Ha! The rag's not worth the dustbin.

Throw the shabby old thing right out of the window
Fling it into the faces of other children!
Ha! Ha! Ha! We laughed and laughed till the tears came!

The Changeling

'Why are you prisoned in these four walls
What the use of these tiny pictures and books?

Your feet are asleep in that patterned carpet
Your body faints in these yellow cushions.

What is this light shut up in a glass case?
And what those dark things hanging before the windows?'

. . . She opened the door and escaped . . .

She pressed her way through the garden hedges
And ran and danced in the dew drenched paddock.

A shrill cold wind blew above the stars,
She felt her arms were changing into wings.

'O, please I should like to fly above the stars,
And fill my throat with your shrill-cold laughter.

I cannot go back to my four wall prison
I yearn and yearn to be free again.

I am wild and cold! I have no love heart
My beating wings have lost their feathers'.

.   .   .

'<u>You</u> cannot fly – weeping your laughter'.

Thought Dreams

A passion vine twists over the fence,
Like white birds the blossoms among the leaves

O, no, they are like white shells
Afloat on the crest of a sea wave.

The passion vine trembles as though it will break
Just like a wave – spilling its shining treasure
Over the desolate shores of my darkened garden.

. . A passion vine twists over the fence
Like faint thoughts the blossoms among the leaves.

O, yes, they are like faint thoughts
Afloat on the crest of my sorrow.

The passion vine trembles as though it will break
Just like my sorrow – spilling its fainting treasure
Over the desolate shores of my darkened heart.

To K.M.

She is a bird.
Green is her body and her wings are tawny.
She is the strange sport of her wild sea mother
Who fell in love with a bit of bracken
Wind wrenched – and flung into her bosom.
Her body cries out in weariness – but her wings never tire.
Her body quivers under a single rain drop
She is frightened to death of the wind in the keyhole;
The smallest bramble thorn pierces its heart;
It is seared by the sun and frozen by the moon.
It laughs and weeps with the wind changed.
'Tis bruised by a floating bubble –
The shadow of a cloud stifles its breath.
'Set me free; let me be', cries her body.
Up and down beat her wings
Over the roofs of cities
Over the tops of mountains
Over the desert shifting sands
Over the scornful face of her lawless mother
Over the turbulent forests where bracken is wind wrenched.

'A moment – a moment . . . I die'.

Up and up beat her wings.

Collection Ends

Limbo

A wreath of pipe smoke rising in a ring;
A tin clock ticking hollow on a shelf;
Outside a ceaseless hammer-hammering;
Next door shrill children's voices – and myself.
The ticking is of dead men's bleaching jaws
Wearily wagging in eternity,
Marking the measure of the stroke and pause
Of Death forging new sickles endlessly.
The smoke is all my little vapour seal
That flickers in a sudden gust of air,
Wearily seeking for a long-lost goal,
A goal that it shall find not anywhere,
Nor find a home for all its wandering.
The voices are the past calling to me
From some old world of toil and hammering
Across dim frozen wastes of icy sea.
The clock ticks on. The rhythmic hammer noise beats
Beats on. The pipe smoke writhes on overhead
Terribly still. The piercing children's voice
Stabs on relentless. Living, I am dead.

'The world is beautiful tonight'

The world is beautiful tonight
So many stars shine in the sky,
And homeward, lightly hand in hand
The happy people pass me by

I lose my way down every path
I stumble over every stone

And every gate and every door
Is locked 'gainst me alone.

Mr. Richard Le Gallienne

Lush and thickly green,
Ah! why must I think of graves!
Of lovers that might have been,
Under these swinging waves.

My sad soul could not rest
Till April knocked my door,
Leaning her delicate breast
Over me – as of yore.

She cried – 'Beloved, see
The apple-blossom fall
Like angels' feathers a-free
From winter's barren pall.

Mr. Alfred Austin

Droop ye no more – ye stalwart oaken trees,
For mourning time is spent and put away –
Red, white and blue unfurls, the morning breeze
Bring leaves – strew leaves for Coronation Day.

And thrill along your mighty, crusted bark,
King George, our Sailor King, goes to be crowned,
Your limbs have nursed his navy – the long mark
Of his wide Empire by your arms is bound.

Bud roses! scatter at the matron feet
Of his proud consort, Mary, all your bloom.
Let Englishman the bronzed Colonial meet
In brotherhood – and weave upon the loom

Of this great Empire stronger, deeper ties –
Ties that shall hold 11,000 miles.
Perhaps in some far Heaven of the skies
Edward the Peace-maker looks down and smiles.

Love Cycle

Soprano: MISS KATHERINE TYNAN.

Spring i' the wood!
And the aconites frail
Cold all a' tremble
In this wild gale.
The snowdrop, the daffodil, hyacinth flower,
Posy the earth in a colourful shower.
Spring i' the wood!

Love i' the wood!
And my love all pale,
White limbs a' flutter
In this wild gale.
'Do you care?' 'Would you dare?' and 'I know
      a sweet bower.'
So I whispered my love in that riotous hour.
Love i' the wood!

Contralto: MRS. E. NESBIT.

Now leaps the sun on his own spears and dies!
Across the passionate sky his red blood flies;
The roses crush their mouths upon the breeze
That woos them, and Dusk threads among the trees.

So leapt my love upon her virgin drouth
So stained and passionate scarlet her young mouth;
She crushed upon me all her swooning grace
In silence – and her dark hair hid her face.

Tenor: MR. WILFRID GIBSON.

Ah, no, Beloved, the air is chill,
We dare not climb th' accustomed hill,
We dare not gaze o' th' familiar sea,
And Autumn's skeleton minstrelsy
Jigs i' the bone of the leafless tree.

No, ah Beloved, thy mouth is cold;
We dare not kiss as we kissed of old;
I dare not gaze in the well-known eyes;
My shivering spirit might surprise
An answering shiver, that barren, dies. . . .

Bass: MR. LAURENCE HOUSMAN.

Howl, wind! Thud, hail!
Drive, rain, upon a naked world!
Weave thy pale pall, snow.
(Ah, God, then, is it always so?
Must the year die, *must* the year go?)
The storm clouds shudder, the old winds blow,
And life is oblivion – hushed.

Break, heart! Beat, hands!
Drive, tears, upon my with'ring breast?
She lies more pale than any snow.
(God, God, then, is it ever so?
And *must* I stay, and *must* she go?)
Despair – tossed, spent, *I* wait below
And mourn my restless rest.

1912

Mirabelle

Breath and bosom aflame
At a name:
Mirabelle, Mirabelle.
Mouth and eyes agape
At a shape,
Hands of me body-warm
At a form:
Mirabelle, Mirabelle.
On the shores of my heart
The pink feet dancing,
From the seas of Desire
The mad waves glancing
At spoil so entrancing,
Foam in their swell:
Mirabelle, Mirabelle, Mirabelle.

'And Mr Wells'

And Mr Wells has got a play upon the English stage.
Now – Arnold Bennett comes from where
They make their pretty songs
I was a draper in my time
And now I am all the rage
My name is Mr H.G. Wells
And Kipps is on the stage.
I'm Arnold Bennett L.S.D.

'She has thrown me the knotted flax'

She has thrown me the knotted flax
It lies concealed in my bosom
It twists about my heart
Sapping the life blood from me
As the rata saps the kauri
As the little clinging tendril
covers the giant kauri
So is the flax on my heart
So would her arms round my body
Cling and crush and enfold me.
Like the flowering rata
Is her young mouth's scarlet.

The Secret

In the profoundest Ocean
There is a rainbow shell,
It is always there, shining most stilly
Under the great storm waves
And under the happy little waves
That the old Greeks called 'ripples of laughter.'
And you listen, the rainbow shell
Sings – in the profoundest ocean.
It is always there, singing most silently!

The Awakening River

The gulls are mad-in-love with the river,
And the river unveils her face and smiles.
In her sleep-brooding eyes they mirror their shining wings.
She lies on silver pillows: the sun leans over her.
He warms and warms her, he kisses and kisses her.
There are sparks in her hair and she stirs in laughter.
Be careful, my beautiful waking one! you will catch on fire.
Wheeling and flying with the foam of the sea on their breasts,
The ineffable mists of the sea clinging to their wild wings
Crying the rapture of the boundless ocean
The gulls are mad-in-love with the river.
Wake! we are the dream thoughts flying from your heart.
Wake! we are the songs of desire flowing from your bosom.

O, I think the sun will lend her his great wings
And the river will fly away to the sea with the mad-in-love birds.

Very Early Spring

The fields are snowbound no longer
There are little blue lakes and flags of tenderest green.
The snow has been caught up into the sky
So many white clouds – and the blue of the sky is cold.
Now the sun walks in the forest
He touches the boughs and stems with his golden fingers
They shiver, and wake from slumber.
Over the barren branches he shakes his yellow curls.
. . . . Yet is the forest full of the sound of tears . . . .
A wind dances over the fields.
Shrill and clear the sound of her waking laughter,
Yet the little blue lakes tremble
And the flags of tenderest green bend and quiver.

1913

Where did you get that hat?

Nuts

I'll never tell
He'll never sell
      Another
      Own brother
Of similar guts
I only say that
I was given my hat
      By one of the nuts

Song of the Camellia Blossoms

Dark dark the leaves of the camellia tree
The flowers of the camellia tree
Are whiter far than snow.
I could drown myself in you
Lose myself in your embrace.

The Last Lover

And so she lay upon her bed
And waited through the night.
He will be coming soon she said
And Oh, his step is light.

How cold you are, how very cold
Cling closely then to me
[One line illegible]

Why do you lie so pale and still
Never a word spoke he.

On her warm bosom his cold head
I'm afraid, afraid, she said.

Scarlet Tulips

Strange flower, half opened, scarlet
So soft to feel and press
My lips upon your petals
Inhaled restlessness

A fever and a longing
Desire that burns in me
A violent scarlet passion
Stirs me so savagely.

Strange flowers half opened, scarlet
Show me your heart of flame
Do you keep it in silken wrapping
I shall find it all the same
I shall kiss your scarlet petals
Till they open your heart for me
And a beautiful tremulous passion

Shall bind us, savagely.

1914

'William (P.G.) is very well'

Writes Dorothy
William (P.G.) is very well
And gravely blithe – you know his way
Talking with woodruff or harebell
And idling all the summer day
As he can well afford to do.
P.G. for that again. For who
Is more Divinely Entitled to.
He rises and breakfasts sharp at seven
Then pastes some fern fronds in his book
Until his milk comes at eleven
With two fresh scones baked by the cook.
And then he paces in the sun
Until we dine at half past one
God and the cook are very good
Laughs William relishing his food
(Sometimes the tears rush to my eyes
How kind he is – and oh, how wise!)
After he sits and reads to me
Until at four we take our tea
My dear, you hardly would believe
That William could so sigh and grieve
Over a simple childish tale
How 'Mary Trod Upon the Snail'
Or 'Little Ernie Lost his Pail'
And then perhaps a good half mile
He walks to get an appetite
For supper which we take at night
In the substantial country style.
By nine he's in bed and fast asleep
Not *snoring* dear, but very deep

Oh deep asleep indeed!
And so on ad. lib. What a Pa-man!

The Meeting

We started speaking
Looked at each other; then turned away.
The tears kept rising to my eyes
But I could not weep
I wanted to take your hand
But my hand trembled.
You kept counting the days
Before we should meet again
But both of us felt in our heart
That we parted for ever and ever.
The ticking of the little clock filled the quiet room
Listen I said: it is so loud
Like a horse galloping on a lonely road.
As loud as that – a horse galloping past in the night.
You shut me up in your arms –
But the sound of the clock stifled our hearts beating.
You said 'I cannot go: all that is living of me
Is here for ever and ever.'
Then you went.
The world changed. The sound of the clock grew fainter
Dwindled away – became a minute thing.
I whispered in the darkness: 'If it stops, I shall die.'

'These be two country women'

These be two
Country women
What a size!
Grand big arms
And round red faces
Big substantial
Sit down places
Great big bosoms
Firm as cheese
Bursting through their country jacket.

Wide big laps
And sturdy knees
Hands outspread
Round and rosy
Hands to hold
A country posy
Or a baby or a lamb
And such eyes!
Stupid, shifty, small and sly
Peeping through a slit of sty
Squinting through a neighbour's placket.

1915

'Most merciful God'

Most merciful God
Look kindly upon
An impudent child
Who wants sitting on.
This evening late
I went to the door
And then to the gate
There were more stars – more
Than I could have expected
Even I!
I was simply amazed
Almighty, August
I was utterly dazed
Omnipotent, Just
In a word I was floored
Lord God of Hosts, Lord!
That at this time of day
They should still blaze away
That Thou hadst not rejected
Or at least circumspected
Their white silver beauty
. . Was it spite . . Was it duty . .?

The Deaf House Agent

That deaf old man!
With his hand to his ear
His hand to his head stood out like a shell
Horny and hollow. He said, 'I can't hear'
He muttered, 'Don't shout,

I can hear very well!'
He mumbled, 'I can't catch a word
I can't follow.'
Then Jack with a voice like a Protestant bell
Roared 'Particulars! Farmhouse! At 10 quid a year!'
'*I* dunno wot place you are talking about,'
Said the deaf old man.
Said Jack, 'What the HELL –'
But the deaf old man took a pin from his desk, picked a piece
of wool the size of a hen's egg from his ear, had a good look
at it, decided in its favour and replaced it in the
aforementioned organ.

'Toujours fatiguée, Madame'?

Toujours fatiguée, Madame?
Oui, toujours fatiguée.
Je ne me lève pas, Victorine; et le courier?
Victorine smiles meaningly, Pas encore passé.

1916

'Twenty to twelve, says our old clock'

Twenty to twelve, says our old clock.
It seems to talk and slyly mock
My hunger and my real distress
At giving way to wickedness.
Oh, say a quarter! Say ten to!
Whirr in the wheezy way you do
Before you strike! But no!
As I have frequently observed,
All clocks are deaf – this hasn't heard.
And, as it is, *grâce à* my guiding,
The brute is fast beyond all hiding.
   It is really only seven
   Minutes past a bare eleven!
Now Jack's got up and made a move . . .
But only to the shelves above.
He's settled down. Oh, what a blow!
I've still a good fifteen to go.
Before the brute has chimèd well,
I may be dead and gone to hell.

To L.H.B.

(1894–1915)

Last night for the first time since you were dead
I walked with you, my brother, in a dream.
We were at home again beside the stream
Fringed with tall berry bushes, white and red.
'Don't touch them: they are poisonous,' I said
But your hand hovered, and I saw a beam

Of strange bright laughter flying round your head
And as you stooped I saw the berries gleam
'Don't you remember? We called them Dead Man's Bread!'
I woke and heard the wind moan and the roar
Of the dark water tumbling on the shore.
Where – where is the path of my dream for my eager feet
By the remembered stream my brother stands
Waiting for me with berries in his hands
'These are my body. Sister, take and eat.'

'Last night for the first time since you were dead'

Last night for the first time since you were dead
I talked with you my brother in a dream,
We were at home again walking by a stream
Fringed with tall berry bushes, white and red –
Don't touch them they are poisoned, I said
But your hand hovered and I saw the gleam
Of strange bright laughter playing round your head.
Don't you remember, we called them dead man's bread?
I woke and heard the wind moan and the roar
Of the dark tumbling water on the shore
Come back, oh darling dear! my brother stands
Waiting for me and holding out his hands
Full of the shining berries.
By the remembered stream my brother stands
Waiting for me and holding out his hands
Full of the berries that I did not eat.

The Gulf

A gulf of silence separates us from each other
I stand at one side of the gulf – you at the other
I cannot see you or hear you – yet know that you are there.
Often I call you by your childish name
And pretend that the echo to my crying is your voice.
How can we bridge the gulf – never by speech or touch.
Once I thought we might fill it quite up with our tears
Now I want to shatter it with our laughter.

Villa Pauline

But Ah! before he came
You were only a name
Four little rooms and cupboard
Without a bone
And I was alone!
Now with your windows wide
Everything from outside
Of sun and flower and loveliness
Come in to hide
To play to laugh on the stairs
To catch unawares
Our childish happiness
And to glide
Through the four little rooms on tiptoe
With lifted finger
Pretending we shall not know
When the shutters are shut
That they still linger
Long long after
Lying close in the dark
He says to me hark
Isn't that laughter?

We are robbers and thieves
Your four little rooms and your cupboard
Are full to the brim
That is why
You stand so trim
Under the starry sky
Our sentinel!
And no one believes
We are more than two
You never will tell!
You will play our game!

Camomile Tea

Outside the sky is light with stars;
There's a hollow roaring from the sea.
And, alas! for the little almond flowers,
The wind is shaking the almond tree.

How little I thought, a year ago,
In that horrible cottage upon the Lee
That he and I should be sitting so
And sipping a cup of camomile tea.

Light as feathers the witches fly,
The horn of the moon is plain to see;
By a firefly under a jonquil flower
A goblin toasts a bumble-bee.

We might be fifty, we might be five,
So snug, so compact, so wise are we!
Under the kitchen-table leg
My knee is pressing against his knee.

Our shutters are shut, the fire is low,
The tap is dripping peacefully;
The saucepan shadows on the wall
Are black and round and plain to see.

The Town Between the Hills

The further the little girl leaped and ran,
The further she longed to be;
The white, white fields of Jonquil flowers
Danced up as high as her knee
And flashed and sparkled before her eyes
Until she could hardly see.
So to the woods went she.

It was quiet in the wood,
It was solemn and grave;
A sound like a wave
Sighed in the tree-tops
And then sighed no more.
But she was brave,
And the sky showed through
A bird egg's blue,
And she saw
A tiny path that was running away
Over the hill to, who can say?
She ran, too.
But there the path broke,
Then the path ended
And would not be mended.

A little old man
Sat on the edge,
Hugging the hedge.
He had a fire
And two eggs in a pan
And a paper poke
Of pepper and salt
So she came to a halt
To watch and admire:
Cunning and nimble was he!
May I help if I can little old man?
Bravo! he said,
You may dine with me.
I've two old eggs
From two white hens
And a loaf from a kind ladie:
Some fresh nutmegs,
Some cutlet ends
In pink and white paper frills:
And – I've – got
A little hot pot
From the town between the Hills.

He nodded his head
And made her a sign
To sit under the spray
Of a trailing vine.

But when the little girl joined her hands
And said the grace she had learnt to say,
The little old man gave two dreadful squeals
And she just saw the flash of his smoking heels
As he tumbled, tumbled
With his two old eggs
From two white hens,
His loaf from a kind ladie,
The fresh nutmegs
The cutlet ends
In the pink and white paper frills
And away rumbled
The little hot-pot,
So much too hot,
From the town between the hills.

Waves

I saw a tiny God
Sitting
Under a bright blue Umbrella
That had white tassels
And forked ribs of gold
Below him His little world
Lay open to the sun
The shadow of His Hat
Lay upon a city
When he stretched forth His hand
A lake became a dark tremble
When he kicked up His foot
It became night in the mountain passes.

But thou art small!
There are gods far greater than thee
They rise and fall
The tumbling gods of the sea.
Can thy Breast heave such sighs
Such hollow savage cries
Such windy breath
Such groaning death
And canst thy arm enfold
The old the cold
The changeless dreadful places
Where the herds
Of horned sea monsters
And the screaming birds
Gather together.

From those silent men
That lie in the pen
Of yon pearly prisons
Canst thou hunt thy prey
Like us canst thou stay
Awaiting thine hour
And then rise like a tower
And crash and shatter?
There are neither trees nor bushes
In my country
Said the Tiny God.
But there are streams
And water falls

And mountain peaks
Covered with lovely weed
There are little shores and safe harbours
Caves for cool, and plains for sun and wind
Lovely is the sound of the rivers
Lovely the flashing brightness
Of the lonely peaks.
I am content.

But Thy kingdom is small
Said the God of the Sea.
Thy kingdom shall fall
We shall not let thee be
Thou art proud
With a loud
Pealing of laughter
He rose and covered
The tiny God's land
With the tip of his hand
With the curl of his fingers
And after – –

The tiny God
Began to cry.

Voices of the Air!

But then there comes that moment rare
When for no cause that I can find
The little voices of the air
Sound above all the sea and wind

The sea and wind do them obey
And singing singing double notes
On double basses – content to play
A droning chord for the little throats.

The little throats that sing and rise
Up into the light with lovely ease
And a kind of magical sweet surprise
To hear and to know themselves for these.

For these little voices, the bee, the fly
The leaf that taps, the pod that breaks,
The breeze in the grass tops bending by,

The shrill quick sound that the insect makes.
The insect hanging upon a stem
And a thread of water dropping among
The mosses, the big rocks and diadem
All the infinite silent song.
The silent song, so faint, so rare
That the heart must not beat nor the quick blood run
To hear the myriad voices of the air

Sanary

Her little hot room looked over the bay
Through a stiff palisade of glinting palms,
And there she would lie in the heat of the day,
Her dark head resting upon her arms,
So quiet, so still, she did not seem
To think, to feel, or even to dream.

The shimmering, blinding web of sea
Hung from the sky and the spider sun
With busy frightening cruelty
Crawled over the sky and spun and spun,
She could see it still when she shut her eyes,
And the little boats caught in the web like flies.

Down below at this idle hour
Nobody walked in the dusty street
A scent of a dying mimosa flower
Lay on the air, but sweet – too sweet.

'Lives like logs of driftwood'

Lives like logs of driftwood
Tossed on a watery main
Other logs encounter
Drift, touch, part again
And so it is with our lives
On life's tempestuous sea
We meet, we greet, we sever
Drifting eternally.

1917

A Victorian Idyll

Yesterday Matilda Mason
In the <u>Parlour</u> by Herself
Broke a <u>Handsome</u> China Basin
Placed upon the Mantelshelf.

Night-Scented Stock

White, white in the milky night
The moon danced over a tree
'Wouldn't it be lovely to swim in the lake!'
Someone whispered to me.

'Oh, do – do – do!' cooed somebody else
And clasped her hands to her chin.
'I should so love to see the white bodies
All the white bodies jump in!'
        –   –

The big dark house hid secretly
Behind the magnolia and the spreading pear-tree
But there was a sound of music – music rippled and ran
Like a lady laughing behind her fan
Laughing and mocking and running away –
Come into the garden – it's as light as day!

'I can't dance to that Hungarian stuff
The rhythm in it is not passionate enough'
Said somebody. 'I absolutely refuse . .'
But he took off his socks and his shoes
And round he spun. 'It's like Hungarian fruit dishes
Hard and bright – a mechanical blue!'

His white feet flicked in the grass like fishes . .
Some one cried: 'I want to dance, too!'

    −   −

But one with a queer russian ballet head
Curled up on a blue wooden bench instead.
And another, shadowy – shadowy and tall
Walked in the shadow of the dark house wall,
Someone beside her. It shone in the gloom,
His round grey hat like a wet mushroom.

    −   −

'Don't you think perhaps . . ' piped someone's flute
'How sweet the flowers smell!' I heard the other say –
Somebody picked a wet, wet pink
Smelled it and threw it away –

'Is the moon a virgin or is she a harlot?'
Asked somebody. Nobody would tell.
The faces and the hands moved in a pattern
As the music rose and fell.

    −   −

In a dancing, mysterious, moon bright pattern
Like flowers nodding under the sea
The music stopped and there was nothing left of them
But the moon dancing over the tree.

    −   −

'Now I am a Plant, a Weed'

Now I am a plant, a weed
Bending and swinging
On a rocky ledge
And now I am long brown grass
Fluttering like flames
I am a reed
And old shell singing
Forever the same
A drift of sedge
A white, white stone
A bone
Until I pass
Into sand again
And spin and blow
To and fro, to and fro

On the edge of the sea
In the fading light . .
  For the light fades.

But if you were to come you would not say
She is not waiting here for me
She has forgotten. Have we not in play
Disguised ourselves as weed and stones and grass
While the strange ships did pass
Gently – gravely – leaving a curl of foam
That uncurled softly about our island home
Bubbles of foam that glittered on the stone
Like rainbows. Look darling! No, they are gone.
And the white sails have melted into the sailing sky . .

'Out in the Garden'

Out in the garden
Out in the windy, swinging dark
Under the trees and over the flower beds
Over the grass and under the hedge borders
Someone is sweeping sweeping
Some old gardener
Out in the windy swinging dark
Someone is secretly putting in order
Someone is creeping creeping

'There is a solemn wind tonight'

There is a solemn wind to-night
That sings of solemn rain
The trees that have been quiet so long
Flutter and start again

The slender trees – the heavy trees
The fruit trees laden and proud
Lift up their branches to the wind
That cries to them so loud.

The little bushes and the plants
Bow to the solemn sound,
And every tiniest weed and grass
Shakes on the quiet ground.

Tragedy

From the towering, opal globes in the street
The crude, white light streams down
On him, blue-eyed, on her, with hair
Like a beautiful, golden crown.

His cigarette glows in the dusk as he slowly paces
And beside him, the woman *shivers* in silks and laces.

'So that mysterious mother, faint with sleep'

So that mysterious mother, faint with sleep,
Had given into her arms her new-born son
And felt upon her bosom the cherished one
Breathe, and stiffen his tiny limbs and rasp.
Her arms became as wings folding him over
Into that lovely pleasaunce, and her heart
Beat like a tiny bell: 'He is my lover,
He is my son, and we shall never part –
Never, never, never, never – But why?'
And she suddenly bowed her head and began to cry.

A Version from Heine

Countess Julia rowed over the Rhine
In a light boat by clear moonshine.
The waiting maid rowed, the Countess said:
'Do you not see the seven young dead
That behind us follow
In the waters shallow?
(*And the dead swim so sadly!*)

They were warriors young and gay
And on my bosom they softly lay
And swore to be true. To plight our troth,
That they should never be false to their oath,
I had them bound
Straightway and drowned.'
(*And the dead swim so sadly!*)

The waiting-maid rowed, but loud laughed she;
It rang through the night so dreadfully:

Till at the side the corpses dip
And dive and waggle a finger-tip;
As though swearing, they bow
With ice-glistening brow.
(*And the dead swim so sadly!*)

1918

Caution

Said the snail,
In delicate armour of silver mail:
'Before too late
I must know my fate,
I must crawl
Along the wall,
Succeed or fall.'
Timid, cautious, one fine morn
She put forth one quivering horn.
Something bit her –
No – hit her.
She expired –
No – retired.
Two ants
Carrying a grain of chaff
Stopped to laugh.
'Come out! Come out!
That hit on the snout
Was only a seed
Blown by some weed.
You haven't begun
To have any fun.'
'But I've had my fright,
That's Life enough – quite!'
Said the snail.

The Butterfly

What a day to be born!
And what a place!
Cried the flowers.

'Mais, tu as de la chance, ma chère!'
Said the wild geranium
Who was very travelled.

The campions, the bluebells
The daisies and buttercups
The bright little eyebright and the white nettle flower
And a thousand others,
All were there to greet her –
And growing so high – so high
(Right up to the sky, thought the butterfly)
On either side of a little lane.
'Only, my dear', breathed an old snail
Who was hugging the underside of a dock leaf
'Don't attempt to cross over.
Keep to this side.
The other side is just the same as this
Believe me – just the same flowers – just the same greenness.
Stay where you are and have your little flutter in Peace'.

That was enough for the butterfly.
What an idea! Never to go out into the open?
Never to venture forth?

To live, creeping up and down this side!
Her wings quivered with scorn.
'Really', said she, 'I am not a snail!'

And away she flew.
But just at that moment a dirty-looking dog
Its mean tail between its legs,
Came loping down the lane.
It just glanced aside at the butterfly – did not bite,
Just gave a feeble snap and ran further.
But she was dead.
Little fleck of cerise and black,
She lay in the dust.
Everybody was sorry except the Bracken
Which never cares about anything, one way or the other.

Strawberries and the Sailing Ship

We sat on the top of the cliff
Overlooking the open sea
Our backs turned to the little town
Each of us had a basket of strawberries
We had just bought them from a dark woman
With quick eyes – berry-finding eyes
They're fresh picked said she from our own garden
The tips of her fingers were stained a bright red!
Heavens what strawberries
Each one was the finest
The perfect berry – the strawberry Absolute
The fruit of our childhood!
The very air came fanning
On strawberry wings
And down below, in the pools
Little children were bathing
With strawberry faces.
Over the blue swinging water
Came a three masted sailing ship
With nine ten eleven sails
Wonderfully beautiful!
She came riding by
As though every sail were taking its fill
Of the sun and the light.
And Oh! how I'd love to be on board said Anne.
The captain was below, but the crew lay about
Idle and handsome –
Have some strawberries we said
Slipping and sliding on the rocking decks
And shaking the baskets.
They ate them in a kind of dream.
And the ship sailed on
Leaving us there in a kind of dream too
With the empty baskets.

Malade

The man in the room next to mine
Has got the same complaint as I
When I wake in the night I hear him turning
And then he coughs

And I cough
And after a silence I cough
And he coughs again –
This goes on for a long time –
Until I feel we are like two roosters
Calling to each other at false dawn
From far away hidden farms

Pic-Nic

When the two women in white
Came down to the lonely beach
She threw away her paintbox
And she threw away her note book
And down they sat on the sand
The tide was low
Before them the weedy rocks
Were like some herd of shabby beasts
Come down to the pool to drink
And staying there – in a kind of stupor
Then she went off and dabbled her legs in a pool
Thinking about the colour of flesh under water
And she crawled into a dark cave
And sat there thinking about her childhood
Then they came back to the beach
And flung themselves down on their bellies
Hiding their heads in their arms
They looked like two swans.

Arrivée

I seem to spend half my life arriving at strange hotels –
And asking if I may go to bed immediately.
And would you mind filling my hot water bottle
Thank you that is delicious.
No. I shan't require anything more –
The strange door shuts upon the stranger
And then I slip down in the sheets
Waiting for the shadows to come out of the corners
And spin a slow, slow web
Over the ugliest wallpaper of all.

Dame Seule

She is little and grey
With a black velvet band round her hair
False teeth
And skinny little hands coming out of frills
Like the frills on cutlets.
As I passed her room one morning
I saw her worked comb and brush bag
And her Common Prayer book
On the frilled table - -
And when she goes to the 'Ladies'
For some obscure reason she wears a little shawl.
At the dinner table, smiling brightly –
This is the first time I have ever travelled alone
And stayed by myself in a strange hotel
But my husband does not mind –
As it is so Very Quiet.
Of course if it were a *gay place*
And she draws in her chin
And the bead chain rises and falls
Upon her vanished bosom.

Verses Writ in a Foreign Bed

Almighty Father of all and Most Celestial Giver
Who hast granted to us thy children a Heart and Lungs and a Liver;
If upon me should descend thy beautiful gift of tongues
Incline not thine Omnipotent ear to my remarks on Lungs.

1919

To Anne Estelle Rice

My darling Anne
After my Plan
For New Year's Day fell through
I gave up hope
Of catching a rope
Which would land me down near you.
Since then I've been
(Pulse one sixteen
Temperature one o three)
Lying in bed
With a wandering head
And a weak, weak cup of tea.
Injections, chère
In my derrière
Driven into a muscular wad
With a needle thick
As a walking stick –
How *can* one believe in God!
Plus – pleurisy
And je vous dis
A head that went off on its own
Rode a circular race
That embraced every place
I ever shall know or have known.
I landed in Spain
Went to China by train
And rounded Cape Horn in a gale
Ate an ice in New York
Caught the boat for Majourke
And went up the Nile for a sail.

Fairy Tale

Now folds the Tree of Day its perfect flowers,
And every bloom becomes a bud again,
Shut and sealed up against the golden showers
Of bees that hover in the velvet hours. . .
   Now a strain
Wild and mournful blown from shadow towers,
Echoed from shadow ships upon the foam,
Proclaims the Queen of Night.
   From their bowers
The dark Princesses fluttering, wing their flight
To their old Mother, in her huge old home.

Covering Wings

Love! Love! Your tenderness,
Your beautiful, watchful ways
Grasp me, fold me, cover me;
I lie in a kind of daze,
Neither asleep nor yet awake,
Neither a bud nor flower.
Brings to-morrow
Joy or sorrow,
The black or the golden hour?

Love! Love! You pity me so!
Chide me, scold me – cry,
'Submit – submit! You must not fight!'
What may I do, then – die?
But, oh – my horror of quiet beds!
How can I longer stay!
'One to be ready,
Two to be steady,
Three to be off and away!'

Darling heart – your gravity!
Your sorrowful, mournful gaze –
'Two bleached roads lie under the moon,
At the parting of the ways.'
But the tiny, tree-thatched, narrow lane,
Isn't it yours and mine?
The blue-bells ring

Hey, Ding-a-Ding, Ding!
And buds are thick on the vine.

Love! Love! grief of my heart!
As a tree droops over a stream
You hush me, lull me, darken me,
The shadow hiding the gleam.
Your drooping and tragical boughs of grace
Are heavy as though with rain.
Run! Run!
Into the sun!
Let us be children again.

Firelight

Playing in the fire and twilight together,
My little son and I,
Suddenly – woefully – I stoop to catch him.
'Try, mother, try!'

Old Nurse Silence lifts a silent finger:
'Hush! cease your play!'
What happened? What in that tiny moment
Flew away?

Tedious Brief Adventure of K.M.

A doctor who came from Jamaica
Said: 'This time I'll mend her or break her
I'll plug her with serum
And if she can't bear 'em
I'll call in the next undertaker.'

His *locum tenens* Doctor Byam
Said: 'Right O, old fellow, let's try 'em
For I'm an adept O
At pumping in strepto
Since I was a surgeon in Siam.'

The patient, who hailed from New Zealing
Said: 'Pray don't consider my feeling
Provided you're certain
'Twill not go on hurtin'
I'll lie here and smile at the ceiling.'

Those two very bloodthirsty men
Injected five million, then ten
But found that the strepto
Had suddenly crept to
Her feet – and the worst happened then!

Any day you may happen to meet
Her alone in the Hampstead High Street
In a box on four wheels
With a whistle that squeals
And her hands do the job of her feet.

Men and Women

'I get on best with women,'
      She laughed and crumbled her cake.
'Men are such unknown country.
      I never know how to take
What they say, nor how they mean it
      And – oh, well they *are* so queer,
So – don't you know! – *so* – this and that.
      You know what I mean, my dear!

'With women it's so much simpler,'
      She laughed and cuddled her muff.
'One doesn't have to keep smiling –
      Now what have I said? – It's enough
To chat over nothing important.
      That *is* such a rest, I find,
In these strenuous days, don't you know, dear?
      They put such a strain on the mind.'

Friendship

When we were charming *Backfisch*
      With curls and velvet bows
We shared a charming kitten
      With tiny velvet toes.

It was so gay and playful;
      It flew like a woolly ball
From my lap to your shoulder –
      And, oh, it was so small,

So warm – and so obedient
      If we cried: 'That's enough!'
It lay and slept between us,
      A purring ball of fluff.

But now that I am thirty
      And she is thirty-one,
I shudder to discover
      How wild our cat has run.

It's bigger than a Tiger,
      Its eyes are jets of flame,
Its claws are gleaming daggers,
      Could it have once been tame?

Take it away; I'm frightened!
      But she, with placid brow,
Cries: 'This is our Kitty-witty!
      Why don't you love her now?'

Sorrowing Love

And again the flowers are come
And the light shakes
And no tiny voice is dumb,
And a bud breaks
On the humble bush and the proud restless tree.
Come with me!

Look, this little flower is pink,
And this one white.
Here's a pearl cup for your drink,
Here's for your delight
A yellow one, sweet with honey.
Here's fairy money
Silver bright
Scattered over the grass
As we pass.

Here's moss. How the smell of it lingers
On my cold fingers!
You shall have no moss. Here's a frail
Hyacinth, deathly pale.
Not for you, not for you.
And the place where they grew

You must promise me not to discover,
My sorrowful lover!
Shall we never be happy again?
Never again play?
In vain – in vain!
Come away!

A Little Girl's Prayer

Grant me the moment, the lovely moment
That I may lean forth to see
The other buds, the other blooms,
The other leaves on the tree:

That I may take into my bosom
The breeze that is like his brother,
But stiller, lighter, whose faint laughter
Echoes the joy of the other.

Above on the blue and white cloud-spaces
There are small clouds at play.
I watch their remote, mysterious play-time
In the other far-away.

Grant I may hear the small birds singing
The song that the silence knows . . .
(The Light and the Shadow whisper together,
The lovely moment grows,

Ripples into the air like water
Away and away without sound,
And the little girl gets up from her praying
On the cold ground.)

Secret Flowers

Is love a light for me? A steady light,
A lamp within whose pallid pool I dream
Over old love-books? Or is it a gleam,
A lantern coming towards me from afar
Down a dark mountain? Is my love a star?
Ah me! so high above – so coldly bright!

The fire dances. Is my love a fire
Leaping down the twilight ruddy and bold?

Nay, I'd be frightened of him. I'm too cold
For quick and eager loving. There's a gold
Sheen on these flower petals as they fold
More truly mine, more like to my desire.

The flower petals fold. They are by the sun
Forgotten. In a shadowy wood they grow
Where the dark trees keep up a to-and-fro
Shadowy waving. Who will watch them shine
When I have dreamed my dream? Ah, darling mine!
Find them, gather them for me one by one.

The New Husband

Some one came to me and said
Forget, forget that you've been wed
Who's your man to leave you be
Ill and cold in a far country
Who's the husband – who's the stone
Could leave a child like you alone.

You're like a leaf caught in the wind
You're like a lamb that's left behind.
When all the flock has pattered away
You're like a pitiful little stray
Kitten that I'd put in my vest
You're like a bird that's fallen from nest.

We've none of us too long to live
Then take me for your man and give
Me all the keys to all your fears
And let me kiss away these tears
Creep close to me. I mean no harm
My darling. Let me make you warm.

I had received that very day
A letter from the Other to say
That in six months – he hoped – no longer
I would be so much better and stronger
That he would close his books and come
With radiant looks to bear me home.

Ha! Ha! Six months, six weeks, six hours
Among these glittering palms and flowers
With Melancholy at my side

For my old nurse and for my guide
Despair – and for my footman Pain –
– I'll never see my home again.

Said my new husband: Little dear
It's time we were away from here
In the road below there waits my carriage
Ready to drive us to our marriage
Within my home the feast is spread
And the maids are baking the bridal bread.

I thought with grief upon that other
But then why should he aught discover
Save that I pined away and died?
So I became the stranger's bride
And every moment however fast
It flies – we live as 'twere our last!

He wrote

Darling Heart if you would make me
Happy, you have found the way.
Write me letters. How they shake me
Thrill me all the common day

With our love. I hear your laughter
Little laughs! I see your look
'They Lived Happy Ever After'
As you close the fairy book.

Work's been nothing but a pleasure
Every silly little word
Dancing to some elfin measure
Piped by a small chuckling bird.

All this love – as though I've tasted
Wine too rare for human food
I have dreamed away and wasted
Just because the news was good.

Where's the pain of counting money
When my little queen is there
In the parlour eating honey
Beautiful beyond compare!

How I love you! You are better.
Does it matter – being apart?

Oh, the love that's in this letter
Feel it, beating like a heart.

Beating out – 'I do adore you'
Now and to Eternity
See me as I stand before you
Happy as you'd have me be.

Don't be sad and don't be lonely
Drive away those awful fears
When they come remember only
How I've suffered these two years.

Darling heart if you must sorrow
Think: 'My pain must be his pain.'
Think: 'He will be sad tomorrow'
And then – make me smile again.

Et Après

When her last breath was taken
And the old miser death had shaken
The last, last glim from her eyes
He retired.
And to the world's surprise
Wrote these inspired, passion-fired
Poems of Sacrifice!
The world said:
'If she had not been dead
(And burièd)
He'd never have written these.
She was hard to please
They're better apart.
Now the stone
Has rolled away from his heart
Now he's come into his own
Alone.'

The Ring

But a tiny ring of gold
Just a link
Wear it, and your heart is sold
. . . Strange to think!

Till it glitters on your hand
You are free
Shall I cast it on the sand
In the sea?

Which was Judas' greatest sin
Kiss or gold?
Love must end where sales begin
I am told.

We will have no ring, no kiss
To deceive.
When you hear the serpent hiss
Think of Eve.

1920

Old-Fashioned Widow's Song

She handed me a gay bouquet
Of roses pulled in the rain,
Delicate beauties frail and cold –
Could roses heal my pain?

She smiled: 'Ah, c'est un triste temps!'
I laughed and answered 'Yes,'
Pressing the roses in my palms.
How could the roses guess?

She sang 'Madame est seule?' Her eye
Snapped like a rain-washed berry.
How could the solemn roses tell
Which of us was more merry?

She turned to go: she stopped to chat;
'Adieu,' at last she cried.
'Mille mercis pour ces jolies fleurs!' . . .
At that the roses died.

The petals drooped, the petals fell,
The leaves hung crisped and curled.
And I stood holding my dead bouquet
In a dead world.

Sunset

A beam of light was shaken out of the sky
On to the brimming tide, and there it lay
Palely tossing like a creature condemned to die
Who has loved the bright day.

'Ah, who are these that wing through the shadowy air'
She cries, in agony. 'Are they coming for me?'
The big waves croon to her: 'Hush now! There–now–there!
There is nothing to see.'

But her white arms lift to cover her shining head
And she presses close to the waves to make herself small. . .
On their listless knees the beam of light lies dead
And the birds of shadow fall.

'By all the laws of the M. & P.'

By all the laws of the M. & P.
This book is bound to belong to me.
Besides I am sure that you agree
I am the English Anton T.

1921

Winter Bird

My bird, my darling,
Calling through the cold of afternoon –
Those round, bright notes,
Each one so perfect
Shaken from the other and yet
Hanging together in flashing clusters!
The small soft flowers and the ripe fruit
All are gathered.
It is the season now of nuts and berries
And round bright flashing drops
On the frozen grass.

1922

The Wounded Bird

In the wide bed
Under the green embroidered quilt
With flowers and leaves always in soft motion
She is like a wounded bird resting on a pool.

The hunter threw his dart
And hit her breast,
Hit her, but did not kill.
O my wings, lift me – lift me
I am not dreadfully hurt!
Down she dropped and was still.

Kind people come to the edge of the pool with baskets
'Of course what the poor bird wants is plenty of food!'
Their bags and pockets are crammed almost to bursting
With dinner scrapings and scraps from the servants' lunch.
Oh! how pleased they are to be really *giving*!
'In the past, you know you know, you were always so fly-away
So seldom came to the window-sill, so rarely
Shared the delicious crumbs thrown into the yard.
Here is a delicate fragment and here a tit-bit
As good as new. And here's a morsel of relish
And cake and bread and bread and bread and bread.'

At night – in the wide bed
With the leaves and flowers
Gently weaving in the darkness
She is like a wounded bird at rest on a pool.
Timidly, timidly she lifts her head from her wing.
In the sky there are two stars
Floating, shining –

Oh, waters – do not cover me!
I would look long and long at those beautiful stars!
O my wings – lift me – lift me
I am not so dreadfully hurt . . .

Notes

Poem titles
Where no title is supplied by KM, we have created one using part or all of the first line of the poem and placed it in quotation marks.
[. . .] or **[?]** in a poem indicates an illegible word or phrase.

Abbreviations
The following frequently used names and texts are abbreviated thus in the Notes:

CW1, CW2
Gerri Kimber and Vincent O'Sullivan, eds, *The Edinburgh Edition of the Collected Works of Katherine Mansfield: Vols 1 and 2 – The Collected Fiction* (Edinburgh: Edinburgh University Press, 2012)

CW3
Gerri Kimber and Angela Smith, eds, *The Edinburgh Edition of the Collected Works of Katherine Mansfield: Vol. 3 – The Poetry and Critical Writings* (Edinburgh: Edinburgh University Press, 2014)

CW4
Gerri Kimber and Claire Davison, eds, *The Edinburgh Edition of the Collected Works of Katherine Mansfield: Vol. 4 – The Diaries, including Miscellaneous Works* (Edinburgh: Edinburgh University Press, 2016)

JMM
John Middleton Murry

KM
Katherine Mansfield

L1, L2, L3, L4, L5
Vincent O'Sullivan and Margaret Scott, eds, *The Collected Letters of Katherine Mansfield*, 5 vols (Oxford: Clarendon Press, 1984–2008)

1903

Collection: *Little Fronds*

In her memoirs of KM, Ida Baker describes how 'Katherine kept a number of poems in a green notebook and drew large designs of curving, half-open fern fronds on the cover.' See Ida Baker, *Katherine Mansfield: The Memories of LM* (London: Michael Joseph, 1971), p. 36. This poem and the next seventeen in total, ending with 'Farewell', comprise the contents of that little handwritten booklet. It is titled 'Little Fronds', signed 'Kathleen Beauchamp' and 'Dedicated to D———. Ake, Ake Aroha' (Maori. 'Love forever'). Many of the poems reflect the influence of school hymns and prayers, and the medieval archaisms of mid to late nineteenth-century Victorian romantic verse, but KM's later delight in pastiche can often be perceived too.

The leaves of ferns are commonly referred to as fronds. In the mid- to late nineteenth century, there was a vogue for feathery-leafed plants (referred to as 'pteridomania'), whether as items of cultivation, collection or home decoration. The fashion also influenced painting, studio decoration for portrait photography and decorative arts – woodwork, stucco and stained glass.

The Sea

There is an obvious biographical influence in this and KM's other early sea poems, since the composition dates from during or just after her first momentous voyage from New Zealand to England, January to March 1903. However, equally influential was the powerful, pantheistic 'oceanic consciousness' in the arts (poetry, music, painting) in the mid to late nineteenth century, which would undoubtedly have shaped KM's imaginative response to her environment.

The Three Monarchs

Like 'The Springtime' (see below, p. 15), the poem is an interesting mixture of pastoral nursery rhyme, ballad form and classical allegory, about the cycle of the seasons. However, the underlying gloom of the verse which rises to the surface in the two final stanzas hints more at German high Romanticism – such as KM was encountering in Heine's verse. See, for example, his *Book of Songs*.

Music

According to many classical philosophers, including Pythagoras (to whom the concept is often attributed), the planets were connected by the harmonious sounds they emitted, ensuring the balance and proportion of the universe. Not in itself audible, this music of the universe was at the basis of many esoteric theories that persisted until the end of the Renaissance.

A Fragment

However genteel and conventionally religious in its expression of wonder, the unexpected breaking of syntactic patterns and regular metre, along with the discrepancy between title and surface contentment, point to the more subtle undercurrents of this short poem.

Love's Entreaty

KM adapted this poem and 'Night' as the lyrics for a song, set to music by her sister, Vera Beauchamp. They were published as songs by Bote and Bock (Berlin) in 1904.

(l. 11) Even in the nineteenth century, 'I'd reck not' was becoming a dated expression, meaning 'I would not care about'. KM's use of grammatical, lexical and syntactic archaisms, which are in keeping with the pastoral and high Romantic medievalisms popular in sentimental verse, also shows the apprentice stylist learning to imitate the idioms and inflexions of former times and other styles.

Night

Published as song lyrics, and set to music by Vera Beauchamp, in 1904. See 'Love's Entreaty' above.

To M

Almost certainly Maata Mahupuku (also known as Martha Grace), with whom KM had recently formed a close friendship at school in Wellington.

Battle Hymn

This poem offers a fine example of KM's evolving penchant, even as a girl, for thinly disguised pastiche, doubtless part of her poetic apprenticeship, learning her art by borrowing and trying out the established styles of the poetic canon. Here the clear echoes of uplifting hymns in the Wesleyan tradition are undercut in the final line of each stanza by bathos and common sense.

The Chief's Bombay Tiger

An inscription alongside a draft version of this poem: 'Written on S. S. Niwaru', shows that it was written during the voyage to London, January to March 1903.

To Ping Pong by J. E. C.

This mock-elevated ode to ping pong (table tennis) is a good example of KM's fast-developing wit. It is also one of the first examples of her delight in speaking in other voices – here parodying the idiom of a young English gentleman. It was probably penned whilst on board ship.

To a Little Child

Despite its initial tenderly lyrical address, this poem rapidly gives way to a disarming pastiche of sentimental, late Romantic verses of mourning.

In the Darkness

C. A. Hankin's *Katherine Mansfield and Her Confessional Stories* (London: Macmillan, 1982, p. 7) offers a variant for the opening line of the third stanza: 'Granny darling, then I want you'. The much more evasive 'O my darling' thus effaces a more self-pityingly autobiographical content, and invites allegorical and intertextual echoes such as Charles Lamb's 'Blindness' or Colley Cibber's 'The Blind Boy', as well as numerous uplifting verses on blind children to be found in nineteenth-century collections of children's verse. See, for example, Henry Coates's 1879 *Children's Book of Poetry*.

The Springtime

Like 'The Three Monarchs' (see above, p. 10), the poem is an interesting mixture of pastoral nursery rhyme, ballad form and classical allegory, depicting the cycle of the seasons.

To Grace

Possibly another reference to Maata Mahupuku, also known as Martha Grace, who would also go to Paris and then London to be educated. Another fine early example of KM adopting a conventionally lyrical, romantic idiom, only to shift abruptly in the closing stanza, and end with bathos and playfulness.

Hope

However short, the poem offers an interesting example of KM's experimenting with counterpoint in its rhythmic structure, breaking an initial rhythmic structure to insert a far shorter line, which, as a result, stands out in sharp relief, creating a contrastive voice and tone.

Farewell

Many late nineteenth-century treasuries of children's verse and stories for young readers ended with farewell verses, bidding goodbye both to the book, and to the years of childhood that it was intended to accompany. KM is thus adopting that same tradition and register to complete her poetry cycle.

An Escapade Undertaken by A Green Raspberry, & A Kidney Bean

A poem clearly inspired by school life at Queen's College, Harley Street, London. Miss Clara Wood was considered quite an institution at the school; since 1841, she had been looking after the girls who boarded with her at 41 Harley Street. By now an elderly lady, she allegedly 'always wore purple, except when she went to the opera, when she wore lavender'. See Elaine Kaye, *A History of Queen's College, London 1848–1972* (London: Chatto & Windus, 1972), pp. 132–3. Miss Barbara Harper was the second mistress who gave 'exciting and unusual English lessons' (Kaye, p. 139).

Twilight

The 'twilight hour' was, of course, a favourite trope in nineteenth-century and fin-de-siècle poetry, and such verses inspired many much-loved Victorian and Edwardian songs (Molloy and Bingham's 'Just a Song at Twilight' being a classic from 1886). One particular example that provides an interesting point of comparison with the short poem here is Heine's 'The Twilight', with a similar end-of-day conversation set at a casement window. In a 1907 notebook entry, KM notes the poetic German term for twilight, 'Abenddämmerung'.

The Old Inkstand

Short as this poetic draft may be, it contains echoes of other texts KM was exploring at the time: namely, Hans Christian Andersen's tale, 'The Pen and the Inkstand', and Thomas Moore's 'Verses to the Poet Crabbe's Inkstand' (1832).

Friendship

The first of two poems with the same title, but with a far looser metrical pattern than the one which follows.

Friendship (2)

A different version of the poem above, in standard ballad form with a clearer narrative structure and romantic theme than the first. It is one of the earliest of KM's poems to suggest the influence of Heine's ballads, and figures in the notebook she was using at the time, just four pages after her transcription of 'Der Tod, das ist die kühle Nacht' [Death is the cool night], a poem by Heine from 'The Homecoming' in his *Book of Songs* (1827).

The Song of my Lady

Like many of KM's early poems, 'The Song of my Lady' reflects the growing nineteenth-century vogue for medieval legends, with a wistful, fairy-tale-like character and narrative frame. The influence of Heine's 'The Homecoming' sequence, in both the respectful address to a lady in the casement and the golden-haired Lorelei, can be felt here. A hint of lurking danger invites comparisons with many tales and legends, but also shows the young KM developing a taste for pastiche and irony.

The Old Year and the New Year

Sent as an enclosure in a letter dated 6 January 1904 to her cousin, Sylvia Payne, though the poem was written on New Year's Eve 1903.

1904

'This is my world, this room of mine'

KM also wrote prose vignettes expressing her delight in the gentle, studious, creative environment of her room at Queen's College, London. See, for example, CW1, pp. 78–82 and CW4, p. 15. The poem gains from being read alongside Hardy's 'The Sun on the Bookcase', also known as 'Student's Love Song' (1870), both in terms of idiom when recording the pleasures of surveying the much-loved study, and the background awareness of ephemerality and passing time.

(l. 9) Gustave Doré (1832–83) was a French artist, engraver and illustrator whose illustrations were reproduced in a wide variety of late nineteenth-century publications, especially anthologies of poetry and tales.

(l. 17) KM was a passionate cellist during her school years, taking lessons with Thomas Trowell, the cellist and composer, father of the gifted twins Arnold ('Tom') and Garnet.

'Dear friend'

KM dedicated this poem to her friend, Isobel Creelman, who left Queen's College to return to Canada in 1904.

(l. 6) *The Orchid* was a highly successful musical play by James Tanner, with music by Ivan Caryll and Lionel Monckton, first staged in London in 1903. Many of the songs, along with the opening 'Chorus', were immensely popular in the years 1903–6.

1906

'What, think you, causes me truest Joy'

The rapturous tones of this prose-poem are reminiscent of Baudelaire and Heine (see, for example, 'A Night in the Cabin' and 'Storm' in Heine's cycle 'The North Sea') – poets who were doubtless in her mind during the long voyage from New Zealand to England.

The Students' Room

Dated 'ii.iii.06' and signed 'K. B.'.

'To those who can understand her'

Like the poem that follows, this short verse may draw on classic images of springtime in the city, but it clearly expresses the awakening of KM's metropolitan consciousness and her delight in the urban environment of London.

A Common Ballad

Dated 'Sabbath Afternoon. – 13.v.06'.
The title of the poem explicitly sets it in the tradition of many of the most popular traditional English nursery rhymes. The 'London Town' reference and the metrical patterns of the first three lines of each stanza are directly reminiscent of the poem 'Which is the Way to London Town'.
(l. 4) Chaddie was the family's nickname for KM's older sister, Charlotte Mary Beauchamp. 'Our sister' refers to KM's eldest sister, Vera Beauchamp.

'I constantly am hearing'

Written aboard the S. S. *Corinthic*, on the return journey to New Zealand in October to December 1906. Having attended an on-board lecture on the Irish poet, Thomas Moore (1779–1852), KM wrote in her notebook, 'If Tom Moore was aboard the Corinthic I fancy his Muse would be inspired to sing' (CW4, p. 26). This poem is a good early example of KM's talent for pastiching.
(l. 7) The medieval name 'Melisand' was rendered a little less obscure in the late nineteenth century, when it was used by Maeterlinck for the heroine of his play *Pelleas and Melisande* (1893), with incidental music by Gabriel Fauré which later inspired his suite (Op. 80). Debussy's opera version (1902) assured the lasting success of the work.
(l. 14) The first two lines of stanza four are from Thomas Moore's 'Scotch Air – Oft in the stilly night', but the tone of her poem, with its gothic insinuations, is very different from Moore's wistful nostalgia. His *Irish Melodies* provide many of the intertextual echoes – including the title – of Joyce's novella 'The Dead', in his story collection *Dubliners* (1914). Stephen Dedalus's brother sings the opening lines of 'Oft in the stilly night' in Joyce's *A Portrait of the Artist as a Young Man* (1916).

Shadows

Written for her Queen's College friend, Hilda Nathan Salinger, in July 1906, just before KM left England to return to New Zealand. Underneath the poem is written: 'To my Friend – in Memory – in Trust – and in Hope', clearly highlighting KM's distress at leaving London and her desire to return as soon as possible.

The [. . .] Child of the Sea

The second word of the title is illegible in the original manuscript.
This is one of the earliest examples of KM's figure of the child poised between the worlds of real life and mythical otherness – both vibrantly alert and human, yet also wistful and spirit-like, with an enchanted,

changeling-like presence. It is worth noting that the figure of the 'Children of the Sea' can be found in 'Night on the Shore' from Heine's poetry sequence 'The North Sea', published in the edition of his *Book of Songs* that KM owned.

1907

Collection: Children's Book of Verse

This collection of poems for children was put together by KM in 1907, with Edith Bendall, a professional artist nine years her senior (with whom she conducted an affair for a short time), providing the illustrations. The manuscript and drawings were sent off to a publisher; nothing came of the project and the illustrations were never returned. We cannot be sure which of these poems were sent off but have grouped them together here.

Claire Tomalin notes that the poems are 'essentially a pastiche of Robert Louis Stevenson's *A Child's Garden of Verses*, with touches of Hans Christian Andersen'. See Claire Tomalin, *Katherine Mansfield: A Secret Life* (London: Viking, 1987), p. 35. Walter de la Mare's *Songs of Childhood* (1902) is another likely source of inspiration, especially his delight in mixing innocent sweetness, wry humour and bathos. Also gaining in popularity in the late nineteenth century, as children's literature developed, were nonsense rhymes and gently irreverent cautionary verses (Lewis Carroll, Edward Lear and Hilaire Belloc being the best known), and it is very likely that KM had encountered examples of these double-edged humorous poems for children alongside the more conventional exalted sentimentality of writing for children in some of the many anthologies then in circulation. Her verses certainly suggest the same pleasure in comic patter and unexpected slips in register and tone.

'The sunlight shone in golden beams'

Despite the conventional, pastoral tones of the title and opening stanza, the poem is a disarmingly disguised macabre fantasy, written from the point of two parents referred to as 'old cronies', thinking about how they would feel if they abandoned their child.

(l. 16) A reference to the classic nursery rhyme 'Three Little Kittens', the best-known version of which is attributed to the American poet Eliza Lee Follen. The first line reads 'Three little kittens they lost their mittens'.

A Young Ladies Version of The Cards

A deck of playing cards as a metaphor for life has been a popular subject for poetry since Walter Raleigh's 'On the Cards and Dice'. The symbolism is traditionally that of diplomatic or political affairs, which might explain why KM composes a version supposedly suitable for 'young ladies'.

The Bath Baby

Bath babies and seemly behaviour from bathing children are further classic motifs from Victorian and Edwardian verse for children – soon to be immortalised in the Mabel Lucie Atwood verse and illustration, 'Please remember, don't forget, / Never leave the bathroom wet.'

(l. 24) Cloying as the expression 'beddy byes' may sound to the contemporary ear, it is interesting to note that the *Oxford English Dictionary* dates its first usage from just 1901.

A Fine Day and A New Hymn

The shift in tones in these two poems is a fine illustration of KM's ability to pastiche and subvert poetic styles and slip effortlessly from lyricism to parody, even as a schoolgirl. 'A Fine Day' starts with the classic tone of children's nature verse and ends with a playful echo of a child's prayer ('Thank you God for Everything'); 'A New Hymn' appears to promise a religious note, only to play with nursery rhymes ('Sing a song of sixpence' and 'Ring a Ring of Roses', the latter ending on the lines 'Attishoo, attishoo, / We all fall down') and nonsense verse. The rest of the collection pursues this constant shift between the lyricism of conventional children's verse and the comic patter of late Victorian nonsense verse.

The Black Monkey

An interesting poem in terms of its use of voice and point of view – KM's speaking persona here is a father, indulgently addressing his young daughter, and joining in her imaginative invention of a fantasy animal that forces her to misbehave.

The Family

The children in this poem have Maori names, even if the poem itself has no clear national identity, and prefigures the perky sing-song style of disarmingly wicked children's verse that flourished much later in the twentieth century. Hinemoa is a classic Maori name for girls, referring back to a beautiful legendary heroine; Tui is not a gender-specific name, and refers also to a common species of native bird; Maina is not a typical name, although it can be found in Maori registries.

'When I was little'

In this poem and the two that follow, the shifts in register hint at the artful blend of caustic humour and pathos that would become a firm characteristic of KM's short-story writing. They also use the hours of the clock as markers of the cycle of human life, a feature that will return in some slightly later poems too.

The Clock

This is one of the earliest instances of KM taking the clock as an everyday object but then building on the metaphor of measured clock time as human lifespan to chart a more encroaching sense of passing time, just as the Elizabethans used the hourglass. In her later poetry, however, the steady ticking of the clock will make the reminder of human ephemerality more ominous.

The Letter

The temperature of a healthy person, measured in degrees Fahrenheit (37.3 degrees centigrade).

The Birthday Present

As in many of KM's verses for children, the *faux-naïf* voice may sound rather whimsical to today's ear, but if read as pastiches of the sometimes saccharine tones of conventional children's verse in the late nineteenth century, the verses prove rather more wry and derisive. The unexpected rhyming pairs (such as 'big' – 'pig') and the syntactic clusters which break the sing-song iambics (such as 'Cook told me they looked like waist bands' or 'Save them till we're married – for'), in order to create sense out of bathos or absurdity, are more reminiscent of some of Lewis Carroll's pastiches in the *Alice* books than of Victorian sentimental verse for children.

The Pillar Box

Subsequently published in *Pall Mall Magazine*, 45: 202, February 1910, p. 300, one of KM's early London publications. Signed 'K. Mansfield'. Edith Bendall possessed an autograph copy where the poem is dedicated 'To E. K. B.' and dated '6.vi.1907'.
(l. 5) Although not frequent occurrences in her work, there are linguistic choices, such as 'nigger' here, which are obviously unpleasant and troubling to the modern ear and mindset. However, they reflect the idiom of the day and its often unquestioning attitude to racial stereotypes. KM is here referring to the broad, generous smiles of minstrels and golliwogs.
(l. 14) 'Letterette' is one of several diminutive forms (such as notelet, epistolet), common in the early twentieth century, to refer to short letters, sometimes sealed and posted without an envelope.

Song by the Window Before Bed

The traditional nursery rhyme 'Twinkle, twinkle little star' is conventionally illustrated by a child kneeling at a window frame looking out at the night sky. From this perspective it is interesting to contrast the expression of innocent wonder in the traditional verse with KM's rather more menacing, earthly alternative.

The Funeral

This poem is an early example of KM's perceptive ear for idiosyncratic language use, accent and mispronunciation, features that were to become a key feature of her later writing style. Here, we see the newly arrived 'little Colonial' picking up on little echoes of a Londoner's voice.

A Little Boy's Dream

One of KM's early publications, published just five days after she left New Zealand, in the *Dominion*, 1: 221, 11 June 1908, p. 5.

Winter Song

While the sufferings of poor children and animals in the harsh months of winter are classic themes in many treasuries of children's verse from the mid to late nineteenth century, KM's version here resists the conventional emotional patterns. Rather than including an uplifting and moralising note, the recurring first and sixth lines reinforce the bleakness, with echoes of the Fool's verses when he accompanies King Lear on the blasted heath.

On a Young Lady's Sixth Anniversary

This poem plays into the late nineteenth- and early twentieth-century delight in coming-of-age poems to mark the growing up of children – as illustrated, for instance, by A. A. Milne's well-known verse, 'When I Was One', in *Now We are Six* (1927).

'Song of the Little White Girl'

There are various types of cordyline shrubs or trees, commonly known as cabbage trees in New Zealand. This poem offers another interesting example of KM's ability, even as a girl, to think outside conventional identities and power structures. The speaking persona addresses a quivering bush, attributing its movements to the distaste it feels when observing a little white girl, when it would have preferred a Maori child.

A Few Rules for Beginners

A playful pastiche of the frequent use of moral or instructive themes in eighteenth- to nineteenth-century children's poetry.

A Day in Bed

Published in the *Lone Hand*, Sydney, 1 October 1909, p. 636, with the third verse omitted. Signed 'K. M. Beauchamp'; illustrated by Ida S. Rintoul.

Opposites

An interesting poem as much for its sociological undertones, observing the links between class, body language and dress codes, as for its subtle subversion of the typical 'model child' poem. However exquisitely behaved the little Patent-Leather-Slipper-Child may be, the mother's voice, which is heard in the final stanza, admits a preference for the dirty, boisterous and spontaneously affectionate child. The anonymously authored 1765 children's classic, *History of Little Goody Two-Shoes*, to which this poem can be related, popularised the figure of a child characterised by her shoes.

A Joyful Song of Five!

The poem captures the excitement of traditional children's birthday parties by citing the first lines or titles of many traditional children's songs and party games.

The Candle Fairy

KM's introduction of fairy themes into her poems and many early short stories is in keeping with the late Victorian interest in fairy worlds – as reflected in such classics as Andrew Lang's books of fairies and folklore. Although later in date, Cicely Mary Barker's much-loved *Flower Fairy* books from the early 1920s frequently recall the tone and style of KM's fairy verse. Her exploration of the fairy world, however, may also be inspired by her readings of Heine. The preface to his *Book of Songs*, for example, clearly sets the tone for the entire collection, which mixes autobiographical references, folklore, vivid evocations of nature, and narrative. This early poem also foreshadows KM's ability to give voice and animation to the objects of the world around her, a firm characteristic of all her later stories.

The Last Thing

This poem is a clear example of KM setting out in the classic tone of uplifting pious verses, before shifting to the much more down-to-earth concerns of a child who runs through her prayers expeditiously so as to go and ask for sweets.

(l. 10) 'Gentle Jesus, meek and mild' is the title and first line of sacred verses composed by Charles Wesley (1707–88), the Methodist leader and hymn writer. The poem was adopted as a popular children's prayer and was set to music in the early twentieth century. KM would later return to this prayer, having Lottie recite and misquote it during the bedtime scene in 'Prelude'.

(l. 11) 'Now I lay me down to sleep' is a classic children's prayer dating from the eighteenth century. The closing line here ('Make me please a better child') is from neither of the two prayers, and suggests a more moralising use of Wesley's uplifting verse before being taken over by more earthly concerns in the final stanza.

A Quarrel

Like 'The Funeral' (see above, p. 37), this poem is noteworthy for its observant reflection of how real, down-to-earth children live, quarrel and speak. The ability to capture the world as if through the child's mind and idiom is one of KM's most striking literary characteristics, creating a style which, in the early twentieth century, was, in fact, extremely innovative.

A Song for Our Real Children

'Way up high in the Cherry Tree' is a traditional song of unknown origin; KM could also be referring to R. L. Stevenson's 'Foreign Lands', which begins, 'Up into the cherry tree, / Who should climb but little me?' from *A Child's Garden of Verses* (1885), a collection whose tone and style had a clear influence throughout her own early apprenticeship, as noted above (p. 149).
(l. 3) 'The busy bee' could refer to 'The Little Busy Bee', a children's song, with lyrics by William McGavin, set to music by George F. Root. Another popular 'Busy Bee' song was Isaac Watts's poem, 'How Doth the Little Busy Bee?', published in his *Divine and Moral Songs for Children* (1719).

Grown Up Talks

Like the earlier entries 'When I was little', 'The Clock' and 'The Letter', this poem anthropomorphises clock times (see above, p. 151).
(l. 12) A reference to the frequently anthologised nursery rhyme, 'What are little boys made of?', usually attributed to Robert Southey (1774–1843). The second verse of Southey's version includes the lines 'What are young women made of; / Sugar and spice and all things nice'.

The Lonesome Child

Published in the *Dominion*, Wellington, 1: 217, 6 June 1908, p. 11. Signed 'Kathleen Beauchamp'.

Evening Song of the Thoughtful Child

This poem gains from being read alongside KM's 1907–8 prose pieces, 'The Thoughtful Child' and 'She and the Boy' (see CW1, pp. 73–6 and pp. 117–22).
Although the themes of this poem are in keeping with those found earlier in this volume, there is a clear evolution of KM's expressive voice and poetic imagination here. The wings, dreams of flight and shadow children create striking echoes of Barrie's *Peter Pan* (1904).

Autumn Song

Like so many of KM's children's verses, this poem reflects her visible delight in shifting register and focus; in this case, the poem slips from classic images of bonny, playful children to the considerably more sombre 'hardened sinner'.

'Out here it is the Summer time'

A reference, perhaps, to the fact that December to February are summer months in New Zealand but winter in England.

'London London I know what I shall do'

The overall rhythmic scheme here suggests KM is initially pastiching the popular Edwardian music-hall song 'Daisy Bell', written by Henry Dacre in 1892, the famous refrain of which is 'Daisy, Daisy, Give me your answer do / I'm half crazy, / All for the love of you.' The poem also expresses her misery at being in New Zealand, when her heart is set on returning to London as soon as possible. She would finally leave New Zealand for the last time on 6 July 1908.

A Fairy Tale

Dated '24.XI.07'.
Olaf is a classic name of kings, princes and heroes in Scandinavian mythology. KM might also have been influenced by Heine's ballad, 'Ritter Olaf', although Olaf in this case is a passionate knight rather than a childlike fairy. The ballad had, however, been set to music by Felix Draeseke and was a popular song in the late nineteenth and early twentieth centuries.

Vignette

The vignette is a short poetic or prose form, blending description and narrative suggestivity, that was particularly popular in late nineteenth-century writing. See CW1 for KM's prose vignettes.

In the Rangitaiki Valley

Almost certainly written at about the time that KM visited Rangitaiki on 27 November 1907, during her camping trip to the Urewera (see CW4, pp. 59–78), although JMM placed it as 1909 in his first collection. Ida Baker's copy of the 1923 *Poems* contains her pencilled annotations, showing that she clearly disagreed with many of JMM's dates and places of composition, as in this instance, where she annotates it 'Earlier'. In this volume, Baker's alternative dating is recorded where appropriate.

Youth

Dated 'December 15th 1907'.

1908

'Red as the wine of forgotten ages'

Two autograph versions of this manuscript exist. Underneath the first is written the word 'Unknown'. Underneath the second is written: 'It cannot be possible to go through all the abandonment of Music and care humanly for anything human afterwards. K. Mansfield, 1908.'

(l. 5) 'Araby' was a romanticised term for the Arabian Peninsula. Already obsolete in the early twentieth century, the expression lingered on in exoticised expressions such as 'the jewels of Araby' and 'the perfumes of Araby'.

The Grandmother

Ida Baker annotates this poem as 'NZ': that is, written before KM's return to England. As poem VIII in the 1910 *Earth Child* sequence confirms, KM was writing 'Little Brother' poems in her much earlier years, and these were doubtless inspired as much by intertextual resonances – such as the poetry by Heine – as by precise memories of her own. These poems recall the death of her beloved Grandma Dyer on 31 December 1906. Having returned to New Zealand on 6 December, KM had not found time to visit her. Her guilt would surely have precipitated these tender memories.

Butterflies

Again, Ida Baker annotates this 'N.Z.': that is, earlier than the date given in JMM's 1923 edition of KM's poems.

Little Brother's Secret

Ida Baker annotates this 'N.Z.': that is, earlier than the date given in JMM's 1923 edition of KM's poems.

The Man with the Wooden Leg

Ida Baker annotates this 'N.Z.': that is, earlier than the date given in JMM's 1923 edition of KM's poems.

(l. 3) Farkey (Farquhar Campbell) Anderson (1850–1926) was a fascinating figure from KM's childhood in Karori. A well-born Englishman and son of a major-general in the Indian Army, Farkey had also spent time in the Indian Army before emigrating to New Zealand in the mid-1880s, where, after a spell in the Armed Constabulary, he became a jobbing gardener in Karori. He never married but always had a soft spot for children. KM exaggerates his infirmity in this poem as, although he was slightly lame, he did not possess a wooden leg. She includes the name 'Anderson' in a list of titles possibly being considered as an anthology collection in a diary entry in December 1914 (see CW4, p. 145).

Little Brother's Story

Ida Baker annotates this 'N.Z.': that is, earlier than the date given in JMM's 1923 edition of KM's poems.

The Candle

Ida Baker annotates this 'N.Z.': that is, earlier than the date given in JMM's 1923 edition of KM's poems. Like the series of poems about her grand-mother and brother above, descriptive details in this poem clearly made their way into 'The Aloe', which KM began drafting in Paris in early 1915, and completed in Bandol, January to March 1916.

By gradually dropping classic rhyming metre here and tending towards free verse, the poem reflects KM's evolution towards prose rather than verse as her most expressive mode of writing.

When I was a Bird

Ida Baker annotates this 'N.Z.': that is, earlier than the date given in JMM's 1923 edition of KM's poems. Although treated playfully here, the theme of the poetic persona as a bird in a tree is directly reminiscent of the overarching leitmotif in the *Earth Child* cycle. It will recur throughout her poetry, sometimes quite playfully, but sometimes as a starkly vulnerable metaphor.

(l. 1) Karaka trees are evergreens, whose name, from Maori, refers to their orange fruit. They grow mostly in coastal regions throughout New Zealand. The karaka trees and the wistful setting in this poem and the one before recall KM's vignette 'Silhouettes', published in 1907 (see CW1, pp. 83–4).

Ave

'Ave' in Latin is an imperative that can be used as a greeting or a farewell. In theme, the poem has clear intertextual echoes of Edgar Allan Poe's poem 'The Raven' (1845), but the metrical patterning and style are in the tradition of English romanticism, and notably Wordsworth's 'Lucy' poems (the fourth of which ends on the lines, 'The memory of what has been, / And never more will be.'). In Poe's 'The Raven', a reader who has been avidly searching for tales of Lenore in books of legends is visited one gloomy night by a mysterious raven who mocks the poetic persona's lyrical quest by repetitively croaking back 'Nevermore'. Poe also wrote a poem of mourning, 'Lenore' (1843), and a short story, 'Eleonora' (1842), similarly dealing with the death and mourning of a lovely maiden who dies.

'Lo I am standing the test'

Like 'Ave', this poem reflects the strong influence of Poe's poetry on KM's creative imagination and poetic style at the time. Its compelling rhythm points to the influence of much late nineteenth-century verse, as well as her musical training. The stylised melodramatic despair of the poetic persona reads more clearly as pastiche when the poem is read alongside the two that follow, which exult in nature, light and the beauties of life as passionately as the preceding poem wallows in darkness and gloom. Nevertheless, these poems reflect KM's clear despair at being in Wellington, when her heart remains in England and London.

Why Love is Blind

Published in 'Christabel', 'Social Gossip', *Free Lance*, 8: 417, 27 June 1908, p. 8. Also written in Edith Bendall's autograph book at about the same time.

Amongst numerous farewell parties organised for KM, before her final departure for London, was an entirely 'violet' tea on 19 June, where, according to the 'Social Gossip' column in the *Free Lance*, 'violets were introduced in every way that ingenious and artistic fancy could devise.' All the guests were asked to write a poem on the theme of the violet, and KM's winning verse was published in the *Free Lance*. See Gerri Kimber, *Katherine Mansfield: The Early Years* (Edinburgh: Edinburgh University Press, 2016), p. 251.

The violet was commonly used as a symbol of remembrance, sincerity and tenderness in Victorian literature, and violet perfumes were very popular towards the end of the century. There was even something of a cult for violets, which is reflected in this short verse. Beyond this contemporary cult for violets, however, KM is also playing with the rich mythological resonances of the flower, since in many Greek myths violets spring up where the gods' or heroes' blood has been shed. For other poems with similar flower symbolism, see below, p. 170.

'Out to the glow of the sunset, brother'

The poem gains from being read alongside KM's later short story, 'The Wind Blows' (1920) (see CW2, pp. 226–9).

In the Tropics

A poem almost certainly written on KM's final journey from New Zealand to England, July to August 1908.

(l. 19) Travellers on ships travelling by night report magical luminescent glows on the water, caused by phosphorus and other elements in the bodies of plant and animal organisms.

'I am quite happy for you see'

The formal organisation of this poem, in three-line stanzas, with a simple *terza rima* rhyming pattern (aaa – bbb – ccc), can be linked back to various lyric poets who were often anthologised or read in schools at the turn of the century; for example, see Robert Herrick's 'Meditation for his Mistress' and Tennyson's 'The Eagle'.

The original manuscript of this poem is written on notepaper headed 'Consulat de France à Smyrne', with the name Käthie Schönfeld at the top. On the reverse side of the paper, KM has written the following:

I do not know why things touch me so, she said – Home Sweet Home. You know I think of all the maudlin – piteously inane – foolishly insipid songs – and its pauses are perpetually punctuated with vociferous nose blowing – people are fools.

[Written underneath in a different coloured ink]

Neither do I

To Pan

Pan is a figure from Greek mythology, who dwells in the forests and mountains. He was originally a pastoral god from Arcadia and came to be seen as the patron of shepherds. He tends to be represented as a goat-like figure with hooves and horns, or sometimes as half-goat, half-man, playing 'pan-pipes' made of reeds. A growth of interest in Pan throughout the nineteenth century reached its zenith in the years 1890–1920, with literary, musical and naturalist resonances (J. M. Barrie's play *Peter Pan* [1904] being a famous example). 'The Great God Pan' was a popular, fin-de-siècle novella by Arthur Machen that may well have fired KM's imagination.
(l. 6) Ralph Waldo Emerson (1803–82) was a major American poet, philosopher and essayist, and the leader of the Transcendentalist movement. George Meredith (1828–1909) was a British poet and novelist, whose memorable portrayals of strong-minded yet endearing female protagonists in novels such as *The Egoist* (1879) and *Diana of the Crossways* (1885) contributed to the evolution of plot and narrative dynamics in late nineteenth-century fiction. George Borrow (1803–81) was a novelist, and the author of a number of highly popular travel narratives; he was also a passionate philologist.

October (To V.M.B.)

Dedicated to KM's eldest sister Vera Margaret Beauchamp. Published in the 'Table Talk' column of the *Daily News* as 'November' on 3 November 1909, and signed 'K. Mansfield'. Compared to much of her earlier verse, which relies on the conventional rhymes, metrical patterns and linguistic turns of phrase of the past, this poem adopts a strikingly modern tone, with its archly urban setting, stark, bold images and free verse. The influence of more contemporary poets such as Arthur Symons, John Davidson and others from 'The Rhymers Club' can be felt here (such as Symons's 'Nora on the Pavement', 'In the Haymarket' or 'The Street-Singer'), poets that, as her reading notebooks of the times make clear, she was avidly reading at this time. See for example, CW4, pp. 39–40.

'You ask me for a picture of my room'

Dated '29/10/08'. The complete shift in tone and style from the free-standing line one to the rest of the poem suggests that these notebook entries may have been intended as two separate poems. The ballad-form poem, which seems to begin 'And through the wood he lightly came', recalls many high Romantic poems of enchantment such as Keats's 'La Belle Dame sans Merci' and Heine's 'Prologue' to his *Book of Songs*.

The motifs of the magic woods, the bird taking wing and enchantment also suggest that ideas for KM's *Earth Child* sequence (see below, p. 165) were already beginning to take shape.

Words for T.W.T.

(Arnold) Thomas Wilberforce Trowell (1887–1966) was an eminent and successful cellist and composer, who, together with his twin brother Garnet (a violinist), left New Zealand in 1903 to study in Germany and Brussels, before settling in London. KM had been infatuated with 'Tom' before falling in love with his twin brother, Garnet, subsequently the father of her still-born child.

A Sad Truth

Also called 'A Song with a Moral' in a version sent to Garnet Trowell. This and the following five poems are dated 'Hull, November 1908'; Garnet received the poems when he was travelling as a violinist with the Moody–Manners Opera Company.

A Song of Summer

The mythical, transformative powers of fairy bread or fairy nectar in fairy tales became a leitmotif in many late Romantic poems such as Keats's 'La Belle Dame sans Merci' (1819) and Christina Rossetti's 'Goblin Market' (1862).

The Winter Fire

Sent in a letter to Garnet Trowell, dated 2 November 1908.

This is one of the poems that best illustrates KM's shift from vignette-like poetic fragments to prose vignettes, sketches and then short stories, and is best read alongside 'The Trio' (pp. 65–6). Despite the blank verse used here, this poem suggests the growing influence of other genres and modes of expression on KM's creative imagination – early cinema and French naturalism, for example, and also Baudelaire's prose-poems (*Le Spleen de Paris*) from 1869. For a detailed discussion of the influence of Baudelaire on KM's writing, see Gerri Kimber, *Katherine Mansfield: The View from France* (Bern/Oxford: Peter Lang, 2008), pp. 101–10. Other motifs achieved here that will go on to become characteristic features of KM's mature writing are the lone woman in impoverished circumstances, sudden surges of memory transforming everyday scenes, and a sensation of liminality, conjured up by the juxtaposition of inner and outer worlds, framed by doors and windows.

The harsh bathos reinforced by an abrupt break in the rhythmic flow and lilt in the final line are reminiscent of some of Symons's harsh transitions in his 'city' poems. See 'Nora on the Pavement' and 'Nerves', for instance. KM's inspiring and unorthodox German master at Queen's College, Walter Rippmann, had introduced her to English and continental European decadents and aesthetes such as Arthur Symons, whose works she read avidly, copying out sections in her reading notebooks (see CW4, p. 98). For KM's creatively rendered recollection of an evening spent at Rippmann's and the fin-de-siècle atmosphere of the setting, see her unfinished novel, *Juliet*, in CW1, p. 52.

In the Church

The stark contrast in this poem (and the other four in the series) between mourning and melancholia on the one hand, and detachment and mordant irony on the other, suggests the influence of Thomas Hardy's poetry. See Hardy's 'The Ivy Wife' or 'Her Immortality', for example, in *Wessex Poems and Other Verses* (1898).

The Lilac Tree

The lilac is a popular feature in literary mythology, dating back to the legend of the nymph Syringa, who was turned into a lilac to escape the advances of Pan. Lilac was also highly popular in Victorian and Edwardian literature and songs. See, for example, Alfred Noyes's poem 'The Barrel-Organ', often performed as a song, in which one of the refrains runs, 'Come down to Kew in lilac-time.'

On the Sea Shore

This powerful evocation of a seascape is reminiscent of many high Romantic evocations of the sea, the most notable being the poems in Heine's 'The North Sea' cycle, included in his *Book of Songs*.

Revelation

This poem has a strong fin-de-siècle flavour in terms of its setting, tone and imagery, reminiscent of Wilde, Symons, Stevenson and many more of KM's favourite authors at the time.

The Trio

Like 'The Winter Fire', the poem is written in blank verse, and doubtless marks KM's gradual shift from narrative poetry to vignettes and poetically intense short stories.
(l. 26) From a song entitled 'A pastoral glee for three voices (The Wreath)', composed by the English composer Joseph Mazzinghi (1765–1844). The singer's opening words are: 'Ye shepherds, tell me, / Tell me, have you seen / My Flora pass this way? / In shape and feature, beauty's queen / In

pastoral array.' Mazzinghi composed chiefly for the stage, but also wrote works for the piano and a number of popular songs.

(l. 32) The poverty and social exclusion of KM's musicians contrasts starkly with the idyllic pastoral innocence of Mazzinghi's song. This is achieved by her harsh descriptive passages, which nevertheless include bleak echoes of the song's lyrics. The shepherds' reply to the first singer's question runs as follows: 'A wreath around her head she wore, / Carnation, lily, lily, rose, / And in her hand a crook she bore, / And sweets her breath compose.'

(ll. 36–43) The harsh, cynical words which the warehouse speaks back to the singers are one of the first instances of KM attributing a speaking voice to the world around her, inanimate objects included: something that would become a characteristic of her later prose writing.

1909

The Arabian Shawl

Ida Baker annotates this 'G.T.', for Garnet Trowell, in her annotated version of JMM's 1923 edition of KM's poems. The poem is a splendid example of KM's sense of voice, and her skill at writing short dramatic sketches.

Sleeping Together

Ida Baker annotates this '1909. Garnet', in her annotated version of JMM's 1923 edition of KM's poems.

The Quarrel (2)

Ida Baker annotates this 'G.T.?' – that is, Garnet Trowell – in her annotated version of JMM's 1923 edition of KM's poems.

Spring Wind in London

Like Shelley's 'The Cloud', the speaking voice of this poem is given to a natural phenomenon – the wind.

'I could find no rest'

Although only a fragment, the lines here anticipate one of the main leitmotifs of KM's *Earth Child* cycle.

(l. 8) In KM's manuscript version of this poem, the stanza breaks off at the end of this line, and KM adds the comment, 'I cannot say it now. Maybe I shall be able to, much later. In an agony I shall suddenly express myself – it is the joy of self expression – – –.'

(ll. 9–38) The second half of this poem is strikingly different in point of view, style and tone, and may well have been intended as a separate, more narrative verse composition. The child's game with the mother and the underlying sense of impending gloom may well have been inspired by

Heine's 'Dream Pictures' cycle in the *Book of Songs*, including his frequent use of the affectionate diminutive 'Mütterchen', which could be translated 'motherling'.

Floryan nachdenklich

Published in the *Saturday Westminster Gazette*, 41: 6129, 18 January 1913, p. 7, and reprinted in the *Dominion*, Wellington, 3 March 1913, p. 11.

(Ger.) 'Floryan – pensive'. KM met the Polish writer Floryan Sobieniowski in Bad Wörishofen in 1909, and they became lovers. He introduced her to an eclectic, bohemian community of Central and East European writers that was to leave a lasting impression on her creative imagination, long after the romance had soured.

To Stanislaw Wyspianski

Published in English as a pamphlet, *To Stanislaw Wyspianski*, by Bertram Rota, September 1938. Written in Bavaria in 1909 when KM was learning Polish with her lover, Sobieniowski. First published in Polish, freely translated with a commentary by Floryan Sobieniowski, as 'Pamieci Stanislawa Wyspianskiego' in *Gazieta poniedzialkowa, Dodatek literacki Swiatecznyo*, 36, 26 December 1910, p. 10. Stanislaw Wyspianski (1869–1907) was a Polish artist, designer, poet and playwright from Krakow, who became one of the figureheads of Polish nationalism. His early death occasioned days of national mourning. KM was introduced to his work by Sobieniowski, also from Krakow, and a close friend of Wyspianski's.

(l. 7) Speaking in her own voice as the colonial subject from New Zealand, KM clearly unites the cause of one small, occupied country with another. Beyond the powerful personal voice, however, these ardent lines are very much in keeping, in tone, vocabulary and rhetorical intensity, with Walt Whitman's *Leaves of Grass*, particularly the panoramic 'Swift wind! Space! My Soul' section, and the overarchingly Messianic voice of a political prophet. As KM's notebooks make clear, she had been reading Whitman's poetry since at least 1907.

(l. 25) The Nazarene is a biblical term used to refer to Jesus, on account of his origins in Nazareth.

1910

Song of Karen the Dancing Child

Ida Baker annotates this 'Rottingdean' – therefore April 1910, in her annotated version of JMM's 1923 edition of KM's poems.

The poem is clearly inspired by Hans Christian Andersen's 'Little Red Shoes', a cautionary tale in which a little adopted orphan chooses to go out dancing in her little red shoes, rather than stay by the bedside of her adoptive mother. Gruesome punishment awaits the child before she can find forgiveness, for the shoes can no longer come off, and continue to dance, even when she chops off her feet.

Loneliness

Published in the *New Age*, 7: 4, 26 May 1910, p. 83. Ida Baker annotates this 'Cheyne Walk, Chelsea' but the publication date makes this scenario impossible, since KM first began renting a flat in Cheyne Walk only in late summer 1910.

The Sea-Child

Published in *Rhythm*, 2: 5, June 1912, p. 1.
Ida Baker says that 'The Sea-Child' and 'Sea' were written in the spring of 1910 in Rottingdean in Sussex, where KM was recovering from an operation (Baker, p. 56). The poem clearly needs to read alongside KM's other poems in a Nordic vein, with their changeling children and partly human sprites of the earth and sea. The wistful, fairy tale-like setting may well have been first inspired by Heine, who likewise made frequent use of the image of the 'child of the sea' or 'children of the sea'. See, for example, 'A Night by the Strand' in his 'The North Sea' cycle, with the figure of the 'Meerkind' (Sea-Child).

Sea Song

Published in *Rhythm*, 2: 14, 15 March 1913, pp. 453–4.
(l. 10) It is worth noting KM's interesting use of accentual verse from this point, with its irregular syllabic patterns, and an underlying two-beat rhythm – aligning the poem more with songs and nursery rhymes than with a written poetic tradition.
(l. 19) 'Wheek' is a rare Old English verb, probably onomatopoeic in origin, meaning 'to squeak', and found mostly in dialectal usage by the early twentieth century.

'A gipsy's camp was in the copse'

Cited in William Orton, *The Last Romantic* (New York, Toronto: Farrar & Rinehart, 1937), p. 273. In the wake of Arnold's 'The Scholar-Gipsy' (1853), many late nineteenth-century poets and essayists idealised and sometimes exoticised gipsies and Romanies on account of their supposedly bohemian, unconventional lifestyles and their preference for roaming the wilds. See, for example, Arthur Symons's 'In Praise of Gypsies' and Zola's 'Souvenirs: XI' in *Contes et nouvelles* (1872), as well as illustrated works such as George Smith's *Gipsy Life* (1880). The tradition clearly has roots well before the late nineteenth century, however, as is shown in nursery rhymes and ballads such as 'The Raggle-Taggle Gypsies', which, despite its subversive undercurrents, was included in a number of anthologies of verse for children.

Collection: *The Earth Child*

This is a poetry sequence that KM submitted for publication in 1910. See the Introduction, pp. 4–5, for further details.

I

The poems which follow are all typed on separate sheets. However, as the numbering indicates for the first twenty-eight, they do invite reading as a poem-cycle, rather than as a compilation of individual works. This feature strengthens a striking comparison with Heine's poem-cycle 'The North Sea', included in his *Book of Songs* (a translation of which had been published by Elkin Mathews), of which KM had at least one copy. See below, p. 180, for her own translation–adaptation of verses by Heine. KM's poem-cycle shares with Heine's the mixture of elfin and human characters, fairy-tale elements in setting and event, the lyrical first-person voice, reflections on childhood, pastoral memories and a sometimes ironical distance. Heine's poetry was much in vogue in early twentieth-century Germany and Central Europe on account of its Romantic anti-authoritarianism. Although KM possibly owed her discovery of Heine's works to Tom Trowell, she may well have encountered them anew through Sobieniowski and his circle, during her stay in Bavaria in 1909.

II

Beyond the 'child-within-the adult voice' that both Coleridge and Blake explored in their early Romantic works, there are striking echoes in image and tone between these closing lines and early sequences from Walt Whitman's 'Song of Myself' in *Leaves of Grass*. Whitman's lyric poem also adopts the loose poem-cycle as a way to bring together different facets of a lyrical 'I' persona and a kaleidoscope of settings, themes and tones. See above, p. 163.

III

The lyrical 'I' takes the reader into an eerie, fantasy world more reminiscent of much late Romantic German and Central and East European poetry – Goethe, Heine, Lermontov, Kuprin and Mickiewicz, for instance. KM's familiarity with such works can be traced back to London, where, since the 1830s, translations of Russian and Central European poetry had circulated, to discussions in the *New Age*, or to Sobieniowski's circle in Germany.

IV

Published in *Rhythm*, 2: 11, December 1912, p. 307, with the title 'Sea' (see note on 'The Sea-Child', p. 164). Sea-songs, including a powerful voice given to the sea, were frequent in late nineteenth-century poetry, particularly from Central and Eastern Europe. Müller's and Heine's sea-cycles are striking examples. The theme and episodic structure of seascape verse were frequently taken up by late Romantic composers, from Liszt to MacDowell, whose works KM had discovered through the Trowells (see above, p. 160). Sea-vignettes and memories of the sea, of course, form a leitmotif in much of her early fictional writing, including the poem 'Sea Song' (see above, p. 164) which recalls the themes, tone and intertextual echoes in many of the sections in this cycle.

V

Published in *Rhythm*, 2: 11, December 1912, p. 36, with the title 'The Opal Dream Cave'. The poem deserves to be read alongside the fairy sequences in Heine's 'Lyrical Intermezzo', included in his *Book of Songs* (see above, p. 153).

VI

Published as 'Very Early Spring' in *Rhythm*, 1: 4, Spring 1912, p. 30.
(l. 2) 'Flags' or 'flag irises' are species of iris – the yellow water iris and the bold purple iris.
(l. 6) Read within the poem-cycle, the imagery of this line is striking in the way it bridges between the literal magic of fairy worlds and the metaphorical magic of memory.

VII

This poem offers another classic image from high Romantic German poetry – the river sprite or river goddess.

VIII

This poem offers a splendid example of KM blending her own or classic memories from childhood with fairy-tale styles, themes and motifs. The figure of Little Brother is, of course, recurrent in many of her more markedly autobiographical poems, although, in each case, the use of capitals gives a more allegorised or fairy-tale tone to the verses.

IX

The motif of the crone or witch spinning or weaving the story of the world is extremely common in mythology and fairy tales, from the Fates in Ancient Greek myth to Anderson and Grimm. In the tone and imagery of these central poems in the sequence, there is a strong echo of Heine's 'Dream Pictures' sequence included in the *Book of Songs*.

X

This poem breaks with the high Romantic vein of those immediately preceding it, creating a stark modern contrast.

XI

Despite the gentle beauty of the individual images in this poem, the under-lying picture it paints of utter loneliness and exclusion reflects a growing maturity in KM's verse, as well as her poignant experience of abandon-ment at this time in her life.

XII

O'Sullivan (p. 90) and subsequently the editors of CW3 mistakenly dated this poem from 1915/16; its appearance in this collection clearly dates it to 1909–10. This poem is an interesting example of KM mixing classic features from myth and fairy tale, evocative high Romantic imagery and a strident, expressionist voice.

XIII

Again, O'Sullivan (p. 90) and the editors of CW3 were clearly mistaken when they suggested this poem dated from 1915/16, as its appearance in this collec-tion clearly dates it to 1909–10. Read within the poem-cycle and in sequence with Poems XII and XIV, possible autobiographical associations are less strik-ing than intertextual echoes – German high Romanticism, Goethe and Heine. KM's epigraph to the overall collection sets the theme of a lost child and a sheltering tree from the outset, in tones reminiscent of Blake as well as Goethe and Heine. See, for example, Heine's 'Homeward Bound' and Goethe's 'The Erl-King', as well as Blake's 'Little Girl Lost' and 'Little Boy Lost'.

XIV

KM's reworking of classic fairy-tale motifs in a modern voice in this poem bears comparison with later writers who went on to make such intertextual rewritings a key feature of their writing – for example, Stevie Smith and Angela Carter.

XV

This poem blends a powerful sense of self-portrait – a bleak reflection of a painfully weary face – and fin-de-siècle, neo-gothic omens in allegorical form.

XVI

The image of the lover keeping vigil for the white sails of the ship announc-ing the return of a loved one recalls 'Tristan and Isolde', even if, in this poem, the lyrical voice would appear to be feminine, and the addressee might be a brother, friend or lover.

XVII

Poems XVII–XIX offer further examples of verses which, read alone, can sound essentially autobiographical, but which, read in sequence, gain a strong mytho-poetical force, particularly in the closing lines of XVII, which prepare for the powerful, passionate idiom of XVIII and XIX.

XVIII

The disparate images of city life, memory, sensory perceptions and hallucinatory vision, along with the suggestively musical, recitative quality of this poem, doubtless reflect KM's keen engagement with the poetry of Walt Whitman in these years.

XIX

The mytho-poetical, epic and high Romantic 'Stürm und Drang' echoes at the end of this particular episode in the sequence, linking it back to the powerful images of poem XII, recall many of the more allegorical, mystical tones of late Symbolist poems by Maeterlinck – see his derhythmatised sequences in *Serres chaudes* (1889), for example.

XX

Published in *Rhythm*, 2: 14, 15 March 1913, p. 471, with the title 'There was a child once', and signed 'By Boris Petrovsky'. Baker (p. 61) claims that the essence of KM's relationship with the writer William Orton was expressed in this poem and that Orton's autobiographical novel, *The Last Romantic* (1937), gives a picture of the time when he knew KM. She deletes the date 1911 in JMM's *Poems* (1923) and writes: 'Orton Cheyne Walk Chelsea'. This would imply the poem was written at some point during the period August 1910 to January 1911, when KM was renting Henry Bishop's flat at 131 Cheyne Walk in Chelsea. In addition to such strong biographical resonances, the poem also reflects the influence of Walt Whitman on KM's poetic imagination and idiom. See, for example, the sequence 'There was a child went forth every day; / And the first object he looked upon, that object he became' from *Leaves of Grass*.

XXI

Motifs found in this poem, which already figured in poems I, II, V and X, reinforce the thematic unity of the collection and its narrative coherence as a poem-cycle. This particular poem offers a fine example of how a single framed image that appears referential and may be a memory is suddenly transformed into myth as the natural world is animated and objects come to life.

XXII

While many poems suggest a Central and Eastern European influence in the high Romantic and mythological resonances, the Russian intertextuality in this section is more explicitly referential: the theme of the sleigh-ride and the bearskin rugs. Tolstoy's memoirs of childhood, for example, include fine descriptions of winter outings by sleigh under bearskin rugs, as do famous episodes in *War and Peace* and *Anna Karenina*. Beyond such obvious classics, the image is, of course, recurrent in Russian literature.

XXIII

Like some of KM's earlier poems featuring shadow children and enchanted settings (see above, p. 46), this episode in the cycle balances precariously between a romantically innocent vision of childhood and an impending sense of decadence and morbidity.

XXIV

This poem contrasts strikingly with the tones of Blake and Grimm's tales in the sections just before, although the shift to a 'little Grandmother' figure maintains the fairy-tale tone and motifs. It also recalls the 'Little Brother' in earlier poems (see above, p. 156). Its tone and gentle lyricism are reminiscent of 'The Grandmother' (see above, p. 52).

XXV

Like poem II, the sensual imagery of this poem bears comparison with Walt Whitman's 'Song of Myself', but the 'bird and nest' motif reintroduces the structural metaphor announced in the initial epigraph. This reinforces a sense of the poem-cycle's unity, in the same way as musical themes reintroduced towards the end of a composition announce the move towards resolution and conclusion after thematic and lyrical developments.

XXVI

The stylised dialogue form in this sequence reinforces the structural counterpointing that characterises the poem-cycle overall, as it interweaves strong biographical features and marked intertextual echoes. KM was also experimenting with dramatic and dialogue forms in her prose fiction in the same years.

XXVII

As specific lexical usage and the men's call later in the poem make clear, the setting here has clearly shifted to New Zealand. KM probably encountered these thematic elements during the Urewera trip, since the group leader was specialised in Maori language and customs (see above, p. 155).
(l. 2) The tui is a striking, black-and-white, tufted bird native to New Zealand, and highly valued by the Maori. In myths and folklore, it is often presented as a spirit that protects the forest.
(l. 15) 'H a e re mai' (Maori): 'Welcome!'

XXVIII

This poem is a fine illustration of KM's mastery of the idiom of fairy tales and folk legends. Despite the seemingly matter-of-fact first line, the setting quickly shifts to that of a highly romanticised, lyrical tale in which human figures and animated objects from the everyday world interact. This is reminiscent of the style of two authors KM favoured at the time – Oscar Wilde and Hans Christian Andersen – but also of mythology in general.

(l. 2) The chrysanthemum is a richly evocative flower, with many mythological associations (of both life and death, and all the seasons of the year) in Greek and Roman myths and Oriental tales, as well as pagan and Christian symbolism.

(l. 21) Wood hyacinths: wild flowers more commonly known as bluebells, but frequently referred to as 'wood hyacinths' in folk tales and legends.

To God the Father

This poem is untitled in KM's original *Earth Child* selection but is well known as 'To God the Father', published in *Rhythm*, 2: 10, November 1912, p. 237, translated from 'Boris Petrovsky'. The direct parallel between the title and the representation of God in the poem, and a stained glass window designed by Stanislaw Wyspianski, 'God the Father: Let it Be' (Polish: 'Bóg Ojciec – Stań się'), in the Franciscan church in Krakow, Poland, was first noted by Gerri Kimber. See Gerri Kimber, 'Mansfield, *Rhythm* and the Émigré Connection', in *Katherine Mansfield and Literary Modernism*, ed. by Janet Wilson, Gerri Kimber and Susan Reid (London: Continuum, 2011), pp. 13–29. The poem's description of an almighty God replicates the image in the stained glass window.

Yesterday in Autumn

There is a striking fin-de-siècle tone in this part of the sequence, doubtless reflecting the strong influence Oscar Wilde, Maeterlinck and Arthur Symons had on KM's literary imagination in her years of apprenticeship. Her inspirational tutor at Queen's College, Walter Rippmann, also played a part in her aesthetic leanings. The chrysanthemum motif follows on from poem XXVIII in the numbered sequence. The rhapsodic prose-poetry recalls Wilde's *Salomé*, for example, and also KM's own early dialogue piece, 'The Yellow Chrysanthemum' (see CW1, pp. 116–19).

Violets

The violet was commonly used as a symbol of remembrance and tenderness in Victorian literature, and violet perfumes were very popular towards the end of the century (see above, p. 158). In this poem, however, KM plays between conventional sentimentality and fin-de-siècle aestheticism when she subverts the sentimental Victorian associations of the flower by having the characters use violets to decorate a skull. She thus creates a macabre interplay within the still-life tradition of the *memento mori*. She may have been aware that 'tête-de-mort' is also the common French name for the antirrhinum, which would accentuate the flower symbolism here.

(l. 9) (Fr.) 'Death's head, skull'.

(l. 15) 'Spring Song' is from Mendelssohn's *Songs without Words*, Opus 62. It is the sixth in a lyrical, seven-piece cycle for piano, sometimes referred to as 'Camberwell Green' since it was composed there during one of Mendelssohn's trips to London. KM also uses Mendelssohn's music as thematic reference and ironic narrative commentary in 'The Singing Lesson' (see CW2, pp. 235–40).

Jangling Memory

Published in *Rhythm*, 2: 12, January 1913, p. 337, by 'Boris Petrovsky'. An odd feature of the poems attributed to Boris Petrovsky, as is the case here, is that they are often written from a female perspective.

The Changeling

Traditionally, a changeling was believed to be a fairy child left in the place of a human child, and such eerie, elfin figures have inspired many tales and legends. Although only specifically named in this poem, the changeling as a leitmotif is recurrent throughout the *Earth Child* sequence, and is indeed latent in the title itself.

(l. 11) The theme of the girl transforming into a bird not only is reminiscent of various tales of metamorphosis from Greek mythology, but also recalls the dénouement of KM's short story, 'A Suburban Fairy Tale' (CW2, pp. 170–3), in which Little B. is transformed from his mundane setting to become one with the birds.

Thought Dreams

Both the title and the imagery here recall prose-poems by Baudelaire that KM had particularly appreciated when a schoolgirl (see above, p. 160).

(l. 1) Passion vine, also referred to as *Passiflora* or passion flower, is a flowering, climbing plant with strong symbolical or allegorical associations. It is named after the Passion of Christ, on account of the flower's resemblance to the crown of thorns. In non-Christian cultures, it is often colloquially known as the clock plant, again on account of its strikingly shaped flowers.

To K.M.

Although outside the numbered poem-cycle, this closing piece with its self-as-other address and the Romantic, poet-as-bird theme is clearly linked in tone, frame and motif to the lyrical part-autobiographical, part-mytho-poetic cycle. As with the opening sections here, it bears comparison with the closing farewell sequences of Whitman's 'Song of Myself'. Read alongside the epigraph and first poem of the series, 'K.M.' also forms a striking framing device for the whole volume as it was submitted to Mathews.

1911

Limbo

Dated 1911 on the typescript. The title of the poem and the bleak solitude of the speaking persona caught between conflicting worlds, spaces and times make it one of the most succinct and most explicit studies of liminality in KM's œuvre, a theme that recurs throughout her poetry, prose vignettes, fiction, correspondence and personal writings.

'The world is beautiful tonight'

Cited in Orton, p. 282. Signed 'K. M. 6 Sept. 1911'.

Mr. Richard Le Gallienne and Mr. Alfred Austin

These poems are part of a pastiche called 'A P.S.A.' (A Pleasant Sunday Afternoon), co-written with Beatrice Hastings and published in the *New Age*, 9: 4, 25 May 1911, p. 95. The pastiche is written as a letter to the editor: 'Sir, – Finding ourselves on Sunday in Ditchling-on-Sea, without any literature, we were driven to rely upon memories of our favourite authors. We forward our summaries for the benefit of your readers who may sometime find themselves in a similar situation.'
Richard Le Gallienne (1866–1947) was a highly prolific poet associated with the Rhymers, who wrote powerful decadent verse in the early years of his career, and indeed published in *The Yellow Book*, a well-known British journal of the 1890s, associated with Aestheticism and Decadence. By the 1910s, however, his verse had come to connote extravagantly predictable forms and styles. Alfred Austin (1835–1913) became Poet Laureate in 1896, although he had previously been mostly appreciated for his sharp pastiches and satires. In later years, his poetic output was essentially limited to topical issues and eulogies of nature.

Love Cycle

One in a series of pastiches written by KM for the *New Age*, 9: 25, 19 October 1911, p. 586: 'Now it came to pass that four of these Sweet English Singers were gathered together in one place. And they took counsel together as to how and in what manner they should beguile a Vacant Half Hour. [. . .] And they stood in a fair sweet line and they sang.' All four 'singers' were, in fact, well-known writers or poets:
(l. 1) Katharine Tynan (1859–1930) was a popular Irish poet and novelist.
(l. 3) The aconite is a woodland flower from the buttercup family.
(l. 16) Edith Nesbit (1858–1924) was a highly successful novelist and writer for children, but also a co-founder of the Fabian Society.
(l. 21) 'drouth': an archaic form of the word 'drought'.
(l. 25) Wilfrid Gibson (1878–1962) was a prolific poet who became associated with the Georgians.

(l. 36) Laurence Housman (1865–1959) was a playwright and illustrator, renowned for his popular fairy tales. He was also an outspoken pacifist.
The considerable skill in this poem resides in the fact that each author's individual style is pastiched in tone, style or imagery.

1912

Mirabelle

First published within KM's short story 'A Marriage of Passion', *New Age*, 10: 19, 7 March 1912, pp. 447–8. There is a striking fin-de-siècle note to this poem, highly reminiscent of the decadent note in Symons's 'La Mélinite' and 'Peau d'Espagne'. 'Mirabelle' is also the name of a highly eroticised female protagonist in a number of French decadent, fin-de-siècle poems and prose-poems, notably in *Le Roi Pausole* (1901) by Pierre Louÿs, a bohemian associate of Francis Carco. The characters in KM's later short story, 'An Indiscreet Journey' (which offers a fictionalised account of her short-lived romance with Carco in 1915), joke flirtatiously about drinking mirabelle, which is also a sweet plum liqueur.

'And Mr Wells'

In this poem and the one that follows, KM writes undisguised pastiche and playfully satirical verse. Her targets here are the two highly successful late Victorian and Edwardian authors, H. G. Wells and Arnold Bennett. H. G. Wells (1866–1946) started out as a draper's apprentice, but by the end of the nineteenth century had become a successful, influential writer and political commentator. KM and Beatrice Hastings parodied the highly detailed realism of his novels in the *New Age*, where Bennett also had a literary column (writing under the pseudonym Jacob Tonson), suggesting the parodies were indeed mischievous rather than vicious. Arnold Bennett (1867–1931) was a highly successful novelist, editor and critic, many of whose stories and novels were set in the Potteries of his youth, recreated as the 'Five Towns'.
(l. 2) Wells's novel *Kipps* (1905) is a rags-to-riches narrative about an aspiring draper's assistant.
(l. 8) L.S.D. stands for pounds, shillings and pence in imperial British currency, in use until decimalisation in 1971.

'She has thrown me the knotted flax'

While all the plants evoked here would have been familiar to KM throughout her childhood years in New Zealand, she became particularly attentive to their powerful beauty during her extended visit to the Urewera in 1907, where she made copious notes about the wild settings, the vegetation and the Maori villages. Such inspiring memories are then transmuted into the startling, sensuous symbolism that both veils and emboldens many of her erotically charged poems.

(l. 5) Kauri trees, also native to New Zealand, can grow to up to 50 metres. Rata trees, which have scarlet flowers, are native to New Zealand. Initially, the sapling rata tree attaches itself to a host tree – such as a kauri – before producing roots and enclosing the host.

(l. 8) New Zealand flax, used by Maori for a wide variety of purposes, can be woven and knotted.

The Secret

KM wrote the poem for Ida Baker in April 1912, 'inscribing it inside the cover of a small book of occult wisdom, which was always one of my treasures' (Baker, p. 68). The occult book in question was a theosophical text entitled *Light on the Path and Karma*, by M. C. Baker's copy is now in the Harry Ransom Center, University of Texas at Austin.

(l. 6) In Greek mythology, the chained Prometheus calls out to the sea, the rivers and the laughing waves of the sea, inviting them to observe his suffering. See, for example, Aeschylus' *Prometheus Bound*, where Prometheus talks of 'the sea waves' innumerable laugh'. The passage is discussed by Symons in his *Studies of the Greek Poets*, Vol. 2.

The Awakening River

Published in *Rhythm*, 1: 4, Spring 1912, p. 30. Signed 'Katherine Mansfield', 'Translated from the Russian of Boris Petrovsky'. See Introduction (p. 5) for details of KM's use of pseudonyms.

Very Early Spring

Published in *Rhythm*, 1: 4. Spring 1912, p. 30, on the same page as 'The Awakening River' and presumably also 'translated from the Russian of Boris Petrovsky by Katherine Mansfield'.

(l. 2) 'Flag' is a common name for certain species of iris.

1913

Where did you get that hat?

JMM's handwritten note on the manuscript states: 'This is a remnant (I think) of the game we played with Goodyear & K. The 3rd person had to make a first verse with the first two (blind) phrases. (22.7.53).' The title is taken from a popular late nineteenth-century music-hall song, composed in 1888 by the American vaudeville artist, J. J. Sullivan. The chorus includes the lines: 'I should like to have one / Just the same as that / Where'er I go they shout "Hello! / Where did you get that hat?"' To be a 'nut', meaning to be eccentric, became a colloquial phrase in about 1900.

Song of the Camellia Blossoms

The camellia flower, with its waxy, sometimes pure white flowers, was a popular symbol of tender affection in the Victorian era, and it also features in many decadent poems. Symons's poem, 'Laus Mortis', explores the symbolism of many popular white flowers, including the camellia. KM's camellia, however, has far more lushly sensual overtones, rather than being mortifying or virginal in the more classic symbolic vein.

The Last Lover

Unlike the series of highly aestheticised flower poems that KM was composing at the time, 'The Last Lover' sees her returning to the more conventional themes, metre and rhyming schemes of romantic ballads and sentimental songs.

Scarlet Tulips

There is a striking return in this poem and the other flower-inspired verses KM wrote in the same months to the fin-de-siècle atmosphere that clearly inspired much of KM's early poetry. See, for example, Symons's 'White Heliotrope' and 'Hallucination'. However, the striking earthy sensuality of the New Zealand-inspired 'Knotted Flax' poem (see above, p. 100) shows KM mixing traditions, styles and influences, rather than working with one single poetic tradition.

1914

'William (P.G.) is very well'

(l. 1) P.G. presumably stands for 'Praise God'.
(l. 2) Dorothy Wordsworth (1771–1855), sister of William, kept detailed, highly evocative accounts of their daily life that attest to her importance concerning the poet's domestic needs and inner harmony. Published in 1897, these accounts became a popular classic in their own right, offering a fine example of Victorian biographical writing outside the monumental tradition. In tone, the poem recalls some of the nonsense verse found in Lewis Carroll's *Alice* books, in particular 'Haddock's Eyes', Carroll's parody of Wordsworth's 'Resolution and Independence', recited by the White Knight in *Through the Looking-Glass* (1871), particularly in lines 23–4.
(l. 32) (Lat.): Shortened from of 'ad libitum', meaning 'at one's pleasure' or 'at liberty'.
A 'Pa-man' was a Beauchamp family expression used to characterise certain men in the family celebrated for their larger-than-life personalities and pioneering spirit, and particularly Harold Beauchamp's father, Arthur, KM's grandfather.

The Meeting

Although highly conventional in theme, in this scene of lovers' parting, foreshadowed by the relentless march of time, KM's use of soundscape and the lone voice, reinforced by bleak free verse, marks a decidedly modern tone. Similarly, the fading tick of the clock alters the more realistically domestic setting and instils more haunted, hallucinatory resonances.

'These be two country women'

While the previous poem relies almost entirely on sound and echo for its effect, this poem is dazzlingly visual but also caricature-like, resembling a cartoon from a satirical magazine such as *Punch*, or a painting by Hogarth.

1915

'Most merciful God'

Despite the opening three lines, which may suggest uplifting Victorian verse, the poem develops into playful bathos in the nonsense tradition, with a parody of biblical imagery and vocabulary, and the sing-song, nursery-rhyme rhythm of accentual verse.

The Deaf House Agent

A poem inspired by KM and JMM's own house-hunting experiences, with a feeling of nonsense-inspired grotesque at the end, reminiscent of the arhythmical last line of 'Humpty Dumpty', as recited by Humpty Dumpty in *Through the Looking-Glass*.
(l. 9) 'Jack' refers to JMM.

'Toujours fatiguée, Madame'?

(Fr.) Is Madame still tired?
Yes, still tired.
I'm not getting up, Victorine; and the post?
Victorine smiles meaningly, Hasn't yet come.

1916

'Twenty to twelve, says our old clock'

As the reference to 'Jack' here implies, the poem doubtless reflects a scene from KM's everyday life, waiting for Jack (JMM) to prepare lunch, and turning the countdown into comic patter in verse. However, leitmotifs such as the relentlessly ticking clock, giving an ominous sense of passing time, hunger and loneliness, also point to the growing anxiety and loneliness expressed in her personal writing and creative work as the years of war, impoverishment and material hardship took their toll.

(l.10) (Fr.) 'thanks to'.

To L.H.B. and 'Last night for the first time since you were dead'

KM's only brother, Leslie Heron Beauchamp, was killed on 6 October 1915, when a faulty hand-grenade, whose use he was demonstrating to his men at Ploegsteert Wood, near the Belgian border town of Messines, blew up in his hand. He was a second lieutenant in the South Lancashire Regiment. Not long after his death, KM wrote in her diary: 'Yes, though he is lying in the middle of a little wood in France and I am still walking upright, and feeling the sun and the wind from the sea, I am just as much dead as he is' (see CW4, p. 171). Haunted by his death until her own in 1923, she would write to Ottoline Morrell in November 1918: 'I keep seeing all these horrors, bathing in them again and again (God knows I don't want to) and then my mind fills with the wretched little picture I have of my brother's grave. What is the meaning of it all?' (L2, p. 290, 17 November 1918).

(l. 15) The final line of 'To L. H. B.' evokes the taking of Communion in Christian church services. *The Book of Common Prayer* gives the injunction 'Take, eat' before the Eucharist, followed by Jesus' words at the Last Supper: 'This is my body which is given for you; do this in remembrance of me' (Luke 22: 19).

The Gulf

Although KM's poetic output declined in the war years, this short poem recalls some of the desolate verse compositions of the previous decade, notably in the *Earth Child* sequence.

Villa Pauline

KM and JMM rented the Villa Pauline in Bandol from the end of December 1915 for three and a half months, a period of great contentment and tenderness, which they remembered fondly later in their lives. JMM writes: 'For the whole of one week we made a practice of sitting together after supper at a very small table in the kitchen and writing verses on a single theme which we had chosen' (*Poems by Katherine Mansfield* (London: Constable), 1923, p. xiii). He cites 'Camomile Tea', 'Waves', 'The Town Between the Hills', 'Voices of the Air!', 'Sanary' and 'Villa Pauline' as verses inspired by their evenings' entertainment.

Camomile Tea

This poem is a fine illustration of KM's ability to record very precise scenes, settings and events from her everyday world in verse form, and yet compose highly evocative poems as 'slices of life' to which any reader can relate. The precise sense of visual detail and sensual experience is, of course, one of the key characteristics of all her writing, whether in literary prose, letters or poetry.

(l. 6) 'That horrible cottage upon the Lee' is an explicit reference to Rose Tree Cottage, The Lee, where JMM and KM lived temporarily in 1914. The cottage was three miles from the Lawrences' cottage in Chesham. This poem, however, appears to be inspired by the wholly more congenial setting of Bandol.

The Town Between the Hills

The poem is an interesting medley of poetic styles and metres, the nursery-rhyme tradition, decadent tales of the devil arriving unexpectedly in an unlikely setting (see Hall Ruffy's 'The Death of the Devil' in the first issue of *Rhythm*, 1: 1, Summer 1911, pp. 24–8, for instance), and the magical trans-formation of the everyday world to be found in many of KM's fairy tales in prose. See, for example, her story, 'The Green Tree – A Fairy Tale', in CW1, pp. 255–60.

Waves

This poem reads as a fascinating patchwork of many of the themes, styles and tones that KM experimented with throughout her career. The rhap-sodic tone and ocean setting, as well as the enchanted atmosphere and dramatised pantheism, recall some of Heine's poems in 'The North Sea' (included in the *Book of Songs*), while the free verse, which is closer to sprung rhythm in places – especially towards the end of the first stanza, bears comparison with poetic forms that evolved later in the twentieth century: in Sylvia Plath's 'Finisterre', for example.

Voices of the Air!

In JMM's 1923 edition of the poems, 'Voices of the Air!' ends at line 16, creating the effect of a conventional poem in four four-line stanzas. The fifth, far more expressive and rhapsodic, stanza creates a much more experimental, evocative medley of styles. Like many of her most powerful poetic creations, whether in verse or prose, this poem reflects KM's musical awareness and her vivid sense of the resonant soundscapes of the world around her. Similarly, the attentiveness to minute visual details, often glimpsed in passing, is reminiscent of all her best writing.

Sanary

Sanary-sur-Mer is a town on the Mediterranean coast, close to Bandol. The idiosyncratic extended metaphor of the second stanza reflects KM's ability to transmute the everyday world into a far more artful poetic idiom.

'Lives like logs of driftwood'

This poem appears in a notebook, in the middle of an entry discussing the character of Beryl Fairfield in the story 'The Aloe', which was being written in Bandol at this time.

1917

A Victorian Idyll

This single verse may suggest the beginning of a pastiche, in the style of Hilaire Belloc, whose *Bad Child's Book of Beasts* and *Cautionary Tales for Children*, in rhyming couplets, had enjoyed great popular success at the turn of the century.

Night-Scented Stock

The poem, sent by KM to Lady Ottoline Morrell, contains a tongue-in-cheek evocation of the latter's house-parties at Garsington Manor. From 1915, Ottoline Morrell's often lavish hospitality, with invitations generously extended to all her friends and their acquaintances, became something of a myth in Bloomsbury folklore. However, Garsington was far more than a mere country house for parties. It had a working farm providing employment for a number of conscientious objectors during the war years, and offered refuge for often impoverished artists, exiles and writers. As underlined in the Introduction (see above, pp. 1–2), the poem is a powerfully evocative piece in its own right, irrespective of its biographical allusions. Partly a pastiche of exalted fin-de-siècle impressionism, comic patter and genteel posturing, its powerfully rhapsodic tone and setting transcend ironic effect. Margaret Richardson's collection, *The Buds of Hope* (1839), contains a poem, 'The Night Scented Stock', written in a rather genteel and lofty tone, to which the title may, in part, be an ironic allusion.

(l. 14) As this line emphasises, there are resonances throughout the poem, and particularly in this verse, of Alfred Tennyson's famous song, 'Come into the garden, Maud', from his extended poem-cycle, 'Maud' (1855).

(l. 15) Brahms's 'Hungarian Dances' date back to the years 1870–95, but they became hugely popular outside Germany in the 1910s on account of their association with ragtime.

(l. 23) Since first being brought to Paris by Diaghilev in 1909, the Ballets Russes had enjoyed tremendous success on the stages of Western Europe and North America, bringing new choreographic styles, vibrant settings, Eastern European folk tales and often bold experimental music to public attention.

(l. 33) Possibly an ironic reference to the anti-Romantic idiom explored in T. S. Eliot's 'Love Song of J. Alfred Prufrock', 'Rhapsody on a Windy Night' and 'Conversation Galante', all of which had been published individually by 1917, although they were not anthologised until 1920 in *Prufrock and Other Observations*.

'Now I am a Plant, a Weed'

The oneiric opening section of the poem may well be inspired by the vogue for 'interpretative dance' in the early years of the century, often associated with the bold, evocative dancing style of Isadora Duncan. Interpretative dance uses the body to translate emotion, the natural world, fantasy or vision into dramatic movement and visual rhythm. Dalcroze eurhythmics, which became very fashionable at this time, was another form of interpretative dance.

'Out in the Garden'

This poem and the one that follows are far closer to the style of poetry KM was writing in the first decade of the twentieth century, with striking stylistic and intertextual echoes of Stevenson's *A Child's Garden of Verses*. See his 'Windy Nights' and 'The Wind', for example.

'There Is a Solemn Wind Tonight'

Although more conventional in form than KM's bolder poetic compositions from these years, the evocation of the 'solemn wind' recalls the figures of interpretative dancing that were so popular at the time. See the two preceding poems.

'So that mysterious mother, faint with sleep'

(l. 6) A now obsolete spelling of the noun 'pleasance', from the French 'plaisance', meaning a pleasure garden.

A Version from Heine

KM's poem is a careful translation of Heine's 'Pfalzgräfin Jutta' in *Romanzero* (1844), following the German original in syntax, rhythm and rhyming scheme:

> 'Pfalzgräfin Jutta fuhr über den Rhein,
> Im leichten Kahn, bei Mondenschein.
> Die Zofe rudert, die Gräfin spricht:
> "Siehst du die sieben Leichen nicht,
> Die hinter uns kommen
> Einhergeschwommen –
> So traurig schwimmen die Toten!
>
> "Das waren Ritter voll Jugendlust -
> Sie sanken zärtlich an meine Brust
> Und schwuren mir Treue – Zur Sicherheit,
> Daß sie nicht brächen ihren Eid,
> Ließ ich sie ergreifen
> Sogleich und ersäufen –
> So traurig schwimmen die Toten!"
>
> Die Zofe rudert, die Gräfin lacht.
> Das hallt so höhnisch durch die Nacht!

Bis an die Hüfte tauchen hervor
Die Leichen und strecken die Finger empor,
Wie schwörend – Sie nicken
Mit gläsernen Blicken –
So traurig schwimmen die Toten!'

1918

Caution

A striking example of KM's taste for nonsense verse and comic patter, which relies for much of its effect on incongruous rhymes and the consequent shifts into bathos they occasion.

The Butterfly

Despite its deliberately trivial banter and playful tone, the poem reads as a cautionary tale, reminiscent of 'Le Chèvre de M. Séguin' ('Mr Séguin's Goat'), which KM translated for the *New Age* in 1917 (see CW3, pp. 196–201). Encouraged to stay in the safety of a lovely flowery garden, the butterfly scornfully rejects the offer, preferring to venture further afield, only to be caught by a passing dog.
(l. 4) (Fr.) 'You're very fortunate, my dear.'

Strawberries and the Sailing Ship

This and the next four poems were written when KM was staying with the American artist, Anne Estelle Rice, in Looe, Cornwall, in May to June 1918; they also appear in prose versions in CW4, pp. 244–5. Anne Estelle Rice (1877–1959) was a sculptor and artist born in the United States, but who came to Britain and settled there permanently in the 1910s. She was one of the artists who contributed to the first issues of *Rhythm*, being at that time the lover of the Scottish Colourist J. D. Fergusson (1874–1961), one of the founders of the little magazine. She and KM became close friends in the war years, and her 1918 painting of KM, in a red dress against a backdrop of flowers, is the best-known portrait of the writer.
This poem is a particularly good example of KM's ability to blend clearly autobiographical, referential details with the themes, structure and leitmotifs of fairy tale. All four poems reflect the ease with which the by-now mature writer adapts the succinct images and evocative settings of poetry, while loosening all conventional metrical and rhythmic patterns until the passages read like prose, but retain the visual organisation of poetry. Her experiments with prose-poems had, of course, begun much earlier in her career, and were doubtless inspired, at least in part, by Aloysius Bertrand and Charles Baudelaire's prose-poetry from the 1840s and 1850s, which, once popularised by Arthur Symons, become popular and influential in Britain.

Malade

Even if no illness is named here, KM's tuberculosis had been diagnosed by the time she wrote this poem.

Pic-Nic

KM also wrote a prose version of this scene, in which the pronoun 'she' is underlined each time, as if make a clearer distinction between the two female figures, the painter and the writer (see CW4, p. 244).

Arrivée

A prose version of the scene, called 'Hotels' (see CW4, p. 243), is more fully punctuated than the poem.

Dame Seule

(Fr.) 'Unaccompanied Lady' / 'Woman on her Own'. Depending on usage, 'dame seule' in French can sound either respectfully chivalrous (and it could thus be used to indicate a 'ladies only' carriage in a train) or poignantly lonely. KM plays on this ambivalence in many of her stories and diary sketches: for example, 'The Little Governess' (1915) (see CW1, pp. 422–33). (l. 8) *The Book of Common Prayer* is the general title for a number of Anglican prayer books, the tradition for which dates back to the English Reformation. As well as setting out the prayers that held the community together, the book introduced many evocative, poetic thoughts that have since become idiomatic in the English language.

Verses Writ in a Foreign Bed

Despite its witty, tongue-in-cheek tone and playful pastiche of a prayer, the poem is, of course, full of pathos, bearing in mind KM had only recently been diagnosed with tuberculosis.

1919

To Anne Estelle Rice

(l. 9) A typical adult pulse rate is 60–80 beats per minute, and a healthy temperature is 98.4 degrees Fahrenheit (37.3 degrees centigrade).
(l. 13) (Fr.) 'my dear'.
(l. 14) (Fr.) 'bottom, buttocks'.
(l. 20) (Fr.) 'I tell you'.
(l. 29) 'Majourke' is a transcription of the French pronunciation of Majorque (Majorca).

Fairy Tale

Published in the *Athenaeum*, 4642, 18 April 1919, p. 199.

KM's poems published in the *Athenaeum* were signed 'Elizabeth Stanley', the name of her paternal grandmother. The fairy motifs and imagery in this poem, like many of the fairy poems written years earlier, recall passages from *A Midsummer Night's Dream*, as well as a Victorian classic, *The Fairy Bower* (1841) by Harriet Mozley.

Covering Wings

Published in the *Athenaeum*, 4643, 25 April 1919, p. 233. Signed 'Elizabeth Stanley'.
The rhythm and leitmotifs of the third stanza recall A. E. Housman's *A Shropshire Lad* poetry-cycle, particularly section 36, 'White in the moon the long road lies.' It is a poem KM knew well, for she quoted it at some length by heart in her diary when staying in Germany (see CW4, pp. 115–16).
(l. 26) 'Hey ding a ding ding' is a line from Shakespeare's song, 'It was a lover and his lass', in *As You Like It*, V, iii, 8.

Firelight

Published in the *Athenaeum*, 4643, 25 April 1919, p. 233. Signed 'Elizabeth Stanley'.

Tedious Brief Adventure of K.M.

Each verse of the poem is in limerick form, and like 'Verses Writ in a Foreign Bed' (see above, p. 126), is a remarkable example of KM's self-deprecating talents, making her prolonged exposure to long medical treatments that promised much and ultimately produced few lasting improvements into a source of witty banter and comic irony.
(l.6) (Lat.) 'stand-in'.
(l. 9) 'Strepto' is presumably a shortened form of 'streptococcus', a form of bacteria responsible for pneumonia and other highly contagious diseases.

Men and Women

As the title of this poem may imply, it is a composition in dramatic monologue, a vividly narrative poetic form that was perfected and popularised by Robert Browning, and which certainly influenced KM's own evolution as a writer. Browning's collection *Men and Women* was published in 1855.

Friendship

Like many of KM's poems in mock sentimental or late Victorian style, in sing-song iambics, this one begins as a charming evocation of a family pet but is gradually permeated by a disarmingly evil tone.
(l. 1) (Ger.) 'Fish for frying'; used metaphorically, it refers to a teenage girl.

Sorrowing Love

Published in the *Athenaeum*, 4647, 23 May 1919, p. 366. Signed 'Elizabeth Stanley'. Like many of KM's flower poems, this one provides a strange blend of childlike fairy tale and chilling fin-de-siècle decadence. This is reinforced by the tone of the second and third stanzas, where the voice of the persona distributing flowers recalls Ophelia's speech in *Hamlet*, IV, v.
(l. 19) In Greek mythology, Apollo created the hyacinth flower from the blood of Hyacinthus, a beautiful youth whom he loved, but who was consequently killed by the jealous god of the wind, Zephyrus.

A Little Girl's Prayer

Published in the *Athenaeum*, 4653, 4 July 1919, p. 552. Signed 'Elizabeth Stanley'.

Secret Flowers

Published in the *Athenaeum*, 4660, 22 August 1919, p. 776. Signed 'Elizabeth Stanley'.
In this poem and others signed 'Elizabeth Stanley', there is a distinct return to the late Victorian idiom that KM had explored in her earlier poetry. The tone and style here recall poems in Stevenson's *A Child's Garden of Verse*, as well as earlier classics found in many late nineteenth-century anthologies and treasuries of verse for children.

The New Husband

Signed 'Elizabeth Stanley' but not published in the *Athenaeum*. This poem was sent on 4 December 1919 by KM, who was at Ospedaletti, to JMM in London, together with 'He wrote' and 'Et Après', asking him to file them for future polishing. The signature 'Elizabeth Stanley' may imply that they were designed for the *Athenaeum*, and might perhaps disguise their more autobiographical resonances, but they read as a bitter attack on JMM's perceived abandonment of her, and he did not publish them until after KM's death. However, even when voicing her inner fears and despair, KM drew inspiration from the poetic traditions she loved. Hardy's *Satires of Circumstance* (1914), which KM's notebooks confirm she read extensively in these years, are a clear intertextual resonance here, especially those recalling the death of his wife, Emma.

He wrote

The dramatic monologue form of this poem, and the adoption of an adoring male persona addressing a more fickle or absent beloved, may recall Browning's 'Andrea del Sarto'. Beyond the camouflage of a male persona, however, this poem captures one of the daily preoccupations and disappointments of KM's life in the years after 1918: impatiently awaiting letters from England. The same desolation is expressed in a large number of letters, stories and notebook records.

(ll. 17-19) Direct intertextual echoes in this stanza come from the nursery rhyme 'Sing a song of sixpence': 'The king was in his counting house counting out his money / The queen was in the parlour eating bread and honey.'

Et Après

Signed 'Elizabeth Stanley'.

(l. 3) 'A glim' is a now obsolete form of the noun 'glimpse' or 'glimmer'.

(l. 7) KM is perhaps making a bitter comparison here between Hardy's inspired poems of love written after the death of his wife, Emma, and her own life, with JMM's devotion coming too late to be of any consolation.

The Ring

Although different in theme, the careful metric patterning of KM's poem recalls Browning's dramatic monologue, 'A Woman's Last Word', first published in 1855, in *Men and Women*. Browning's poem is composed of alternating lines of two and three trochees, whereas KM's poem alternates between trochaic dimeter and tetrameter.

(ll. 9-10) The Gospels of Matthew and Mark both recount that Judas kisses Jesus in the Garden of Gethsemane to identify him and so to betray him to the soldiers who had come to arrest him; he receives thirty pieces of silver in return, a payment that he later returns with shame to the high priests who had commissioned him, before hanging himself.

1920

Old-Fashioned Widow's Song

Published in the *Athenaeum*, 4680, 9 January 1920, p. 42. Signed 'Elizabeth Stanley'. In this and the series of poems that follow, KM is clearly exploring omens of death and lost dreams, drawing on the late Romantic tradition for fairy-tale-like fantasies that end with a chilling awakening, as well as more self-consciously ironic echoes, such as she picks out in Hardy's poetry in her notebooks (see, for example, CW4, pp. 292 and 299).

(l. 5) (Fr.) 'The weather is gloomy.'

(l. 9) (Fr.) 'Is Madame alone?'

(l. 15) (Fr.) 'A thousand thanks for these lovely flowers.'

Sunset

Published in the *Athenaeum*, 4682, 23 January 1920, p. 103. Signed 'Elizabeth Stanley'.

'By all the laws of the M. & P.'

In a notebook entry after this verse, KM wrote: 'God forgive me, Tchehov, for my impertinence' (12 December 1920).

1921

Winter Bird

The conventional, gentle images of the natural world in wintertime in this poem recall the influence of children's poetry and the Georgian poets, notably Stevenson and Walter de la Mare's nature poems for children.

1922

The Wounded Bird

Written in the Hôtel d'Angleterre, Sierre, Switzerland, in July 1922, where KM had moved in the hope that the air would be beneficial to her health. It clearly reflects the desolate frustration of a once freedom-loving, now fragile patient forced to endure the well-meaning intentions of those who come to nurse her.

(ll. 8-9 and final refrain) KM habitually referred to her lungs as her 'wings', and it is therefore poignant to note that these last two poems, written just months before her death, should focus on birds. However, the theme also links back to some of her earliest poetry, notably in the *Earth Child* sequence. In tone and motif, this poem bears comparison with Emily Dickinson's 'Hope is the thing with Feathers' (1891) and Shelley's 'Ode to the West Wind' (1820): 'O lift me as a wave, a leaf, a cloud! I fall upon the thorns of life, I bleed.'

Further Reading

Baker, Ida, *Katherine Mansfield: The Memories of LM* (London: Michael Joseph, 1971).

Hankin, C. A., *Katherine Mansfield and Her Confessional Stories* (London: Macmillan, 1982).

Hardy, Thomas, *Wessex Poems and Other Verses* (London: Harper & Brothers, 1898).

Kaye, Elaine, *A History of Queen's College, London 1848–1972* (London: Chatto & Windus, 1972).

Kimber, Gerri, *Katherine Mansfield: The Early Years* (Edinburgh: Edinburgh University Press, 2016).

—— *Katherine Mansfield: The View from France* (Bern/Oxford: Peter Lang, 2008).

—— 'Mansfield, *Rhythm* and the Émigré Connection' in *Katherine Mansfield and Literary Modernism*, ed. by Janet Wilson, Gerri Kimber and Susan Reid (London: Continuum, 2011), pp. 13–29.

—— and Vincent O'Sullivan, eds, *The Edinburgh Edition of the Collected Works of Katherine Mansfield: Vols 1 and 2 – The Collected Fiction* (Edinburgh: Edinburgh University Press, 2012).

—— and Angela Smith, eds, *The Edinburgh Edition of the Collected Works of Katherine Mansfield: Vol. 3 – The Poetry and Critical Writings* (Edinburgh: Edinburgh University Press, 2014).

—— and Claire Davison, eds, *The Edinburgh Edition of the Collected Works of Katherine Mansfield: Vol. 4 – The Diaries, including Miscellaneous Works* (Edinburgh: Edinburgh University Press, 2016).

Murry, John Middleton, ed., *Poems by Katherine Mansfield* (London: Constable, 1923).

—— ed., *Poems by Katherine Mansfield* (London: Constable, 1930).

Orton, William, *The Last Romantic* (New York, Toronto: Farrar & Rinehart, 1937).

O'Sullivan, Vincent, ed., *Poems of Katherine Mansfield* (Auckland: Oxford University Press, 1988).

—— and Margaret Scott, eds, *The Collected Letters of Katherine Mansfield*, 5 vols (Oxford: Clarendon Press, 1984–2008).

Shaw, Helen, ed., *Dear Lady Ginger: An Exchange of Letters Between Lady Ottoline Morrell and D'Arcy Cresswell* (Oxford: Oxford University Press, 1983).

Tomalin, Claire, *Katherine Mansfield: A Secret Life* (London: Viking, 1987).

First Line Index

Index